Jesus Christ,
My Hope
in Grief

BOOK 3 IN THE *My Journey Home* STUDY SERIES

JESUS CHRIST, *My Hope* IN GRIEF

My Gentle Giant, Victor Carr

RITA CARR

CREATION HOUSE

Jesus Christ, My Hope in Grief: My Gentle Giant, Victor Carr
by Dr. Rita Carr
Published by Creation House
A Charisma Media Company
600 Rinehart Road
Lake Mary, Florida 32746
www.charismamedia.com

This book or parts thereof may not be reproduced in any form, stored in a retrieval system, or transmitted in any form by any means—electronic, mechanical, photocopy, recording, or otherwise—without prior written permission of the publisher, except as provided by United States of America copyright law.

Unless otherwise noted, all Scripture quotations are from King James Version.

Scripture quotations marked NIV are from the Holy Bible, New International Version. Copyright © 1973, 1978, 1984, International Bible Society. Used by permission.

Scripture quotations marked NKJV are from the New King James Version of the Bible. Copyright © 1979, 1980, 1982 by Thomas Nelson, Inc., publishers. Used by permission.

Scripture quotations marked NASB are from the New American Standard Bible. Copyright © 1960, 1962, 1963, 1968, 1971, 1972, 1973, 1975, 1977, 1995 by the Lockman Foundation. Used by permission. (www.Lockman.org)

Design Director: Justin Evans
Cover design by Terry Clifton

Copyright © 2015 by Dr. Rita Carr
All rights reserved.

Visit the author's website: http://www.hopeunlimitedministries.org.

Library of Congress Cataloging-in-Publication Data: 2014953347
International Standard Book Number: 978-1-62136-810-6
E-book International Standard Book Number: 978-1-62136-811-3

While the author has made every effort to provide accurate telephone numbers and Internet addresses at the time of publication, neither the publisher nor the author assumes any responsibility for errors or for changes that occur after publication.

15 16 17 18 19 — 9 8 7 6 5 4 3 2
Printed in the United States of America

Jesus Christ, a faithful companion, will enable you to find continuous strength beyond measure; hope that sustains; peace that surrounds you; grace for each day; and loving and strong arms as He carries you in your journey of grief. God will forever be your sustaining anchor in the midst of the storms of life. Our awesome God is mighty and faithful; His love forever carries us in the pain and sorrows of life. God will never let His children journey alone.

—Love, Rita Carr
(Lamentations 3:20–23)

For God so loved the world that he gave his one and only Son, that whoever believes in him shall not perish but have eternal life.
—John 3:16, niv

I dedicate this book to my Lord and Savior Jesus Christ, for His ways are always perfect. Thank You, Lord, for Your precious gift of salvation.

To Victor, my gentle giant: one day my journey on Earth will end, and I will embrace you with a million kisses. I will see my Heavenly Father face to face. What an eternal rejoicing that will be!

To every lineage of the seed of my generations: may you live a life that greatly glorifies the Lord, seeking to be salt and light to family, neighbors, friends, and a hurting, lost, and dying world. May you be a vessel of salt and light, carrying God's Word to the lost so that, prayerfully, they may be saved and have eternal life. And may you minister hope to those who are hopeless that they will truly know God's great love for them.

To everyone who has experienced the passing of a loved one. May you embrace God's faithfulness, love, grace, strength, and healing. Even greater—if you do not know Jesus Christ as your Lord and Savior, may He become your Redeemer and Healer.

CONTENTS

Introduction ix

1 Victor, God's Gift of Life 1
2 Adolescence 5
3 Adulthood 11
4 Sorrow: *God, Our Comfort in Our Sorrow* 19
5 Denial: *Lord, Embrace Me in the Reality of My Sorrow* 27
6 Anguish: *Lord, Heal My Wounded Emotions* 35
7 Sadness: *Lord, You Are My Hope in My Saddened Heart* 39
8 Loneliness: *Lord, Hold Me Until the Storm Passes Over* 47
9 Seclusion: *Lord, You Are My Hiding Place* 59
10 Disbelief and Shock: *Lord, Is Victor Really Gone?* 67
11 Anger: *Lord, Heal Me in My Anger* 73
12 Worry: *Lord, I Am Afraid and Worried. How Does Life Continue?* 81
13 Longing: *Oh Lord, My Heart Yearns for My Loved One! Will My Life Ever Be the Same?* 89
14 Regret: *Lord, Heal Me of My Regrets* 95
15 Depression: *Lord, Be My Song in the Night* 101
16 Perseverance: *Lord, Be My Strength as I Seek to Move Forward* 115
17 Purpose: *Does My Life Have Purpose? The Void and Emptiness of the Passing of a Loved One* 123

18	Peace: *Lord, You Are My Peace*	131
19	Refuge and Comfort: *Lord, You Are My Refuge and Comfort*	139
20	Joy Beyond Measure: *Lord You are my Joy*	149
21	Our God Reigns!	155
	About the Author	159
	Contact the Author	161

INTRODUCTION

Precious Moments in the Life of Victor Dywon Carr

Jesus Christ, My Hope in Grief reflects cherished and loving moments in the life of my precious son, Victor Carr. He was my gentle giant, and I have seen God's faithfulness throughout his life as he journeyed to his eternal home (2 Cor. 5:8).

The Lord in His awesome love gave me thirty wonderful years with my precious son. Victor was a man of integrity whose love for the Lord continues in the memories and hearts of those who knew him. These precious moments are the cherished treasures of my heart. Until that wonderful day when I see Victor again, I will embrace the precious memories of our years together. With great joy, I will see my son again and my Lord Jesus face to face.

This is also a study guide of God's faithfulness and my personal journey with the Lord as He journeyed with me. He has been my sustaining hope in grief. This study guide also reflects the sustaining strength of God's peace and awesome love. His power will enable us to journey in the greatest storms, heartaches, and sorrows of life. The Lord never leaves His children to journey alone (Heb. 13:5).

The Lord has faithfully journeyed with me after Victor's home-going; it truly has been a sweet time of intimacy with the Father. My hope is that my journey will help bring comfort and hope to you in your journey. The Lord is truly with you.

SUDDENLY

> Why, you do not even know what will happen tomorrow. What is your life? You are a mist that appears for a little while and then vanishes.
> —James 4:14, niv

As Victor prepared to leave that morning in October, I stopped him, put my arms around his broad shoulders, and began to pray for him as I daily did. I prayed that the Lord would protect him from the deer that would dash in front of cars without notice and that he would not have an accident. After praying, I kissed Victor's bearded cheek and hugged him tightly, telling him that I loved him. He kissed my check and said, "Mom, I love you too."

Suddenly, without notice, my life changed on October 11, 2010.

> *Dear Lord,*
>
> *How suddenly like a vapor the life of my son, my gentle giant, passed from this life to eternity. Yet, Father, in Victor's appointed time, You did not leave me alone in my journey of grief. Thank You, Lord. You have seen my tears and comforted my heart in my journey—forever reminding me that You never leave Your children to journey alone.*

It seems like yesterday that my precious son and I were sitting at the kitchen table laughing about the day's events, working together in ministry, or just hanging out. It seems like yesterday that I heard those words, "Mom, do you need help?"—or listened while he shared his journal with me: "Mom, let me share with you what the Lord is showing me." It seems like yesterday that I heard him say, "Mom, I have a problem, pray for me"—or held him and prayed earnestly, seeking God on behalf of my beloved son. It seems like yesterday that Victor's arms were tightly hugging me as he said, "Mom, I love you." Yet there is a day coming when I will feel his loving embrace and hear those words, "I love you," once again. There is coming a day... Until that time, by God's grace, I press on serving our Heavenly Father with all of my heart and breath, seeking to reach a hurting, lost, and dying world as our Heavenly Father gives me strength.

> *Daddy, thank You for my son Victor. Thank You that You are his Messiah, and that he lives with you today. Thank You that this life will pass, and I will see my gentle giant again for all eternity, never again to part. Lord, I will see Your face, and I pray that I will hear you say, "Well done, My good and faithful servant." I love you, Victor. I love You, my Heavenly Father; thank You for Your loving faithfulness! And thank You for loving and saving Victor and giving him eternal life! (John 3:16)*

Chapter 1

VICTOR, GOD'S GIFT OF LIFE

Infancy to Childhood

Victor, my gentle giant and precious son, was born a beautiful bundle of joy! He was my second child. My oldest child, Tondra, was eight years older than Victor. From infancy to toddlerhood, Victor was a bundle of joy, smiles, and giggles. He was a beautiful baby I fondly called "Big Vic" because he would always give me little, wet kisses and big, tight hugs. I so loved kissing his chunky cheeks. What a gift from God!

Two years prior to Victor's birth, I had become a Christian when I received Jesus Christ as my Lord and Savior (see John 3:16). As a young Christian with a child-like faith, I began to ask the Lord for another child, a beautiful baby boy. Sadly, prior to my gentle giant's birth, I suffered a miscarriage.

But God healed my broken heart, and by His wonderful grace, I continued to trust Him for a son. With great gladness and joy on November 22, 1979, God blessed Victor's father and me with a baby boy, Victor Dywon Carr. To my delight, Victor began to smile shortly after being born. What a blessing as the Lord answered my prayers and blessed our lives with this gift! What an awesome God we serve, for there is nothing impossible with Him! (Luke 1:37) What joy when Victor was dedicated to the Lord.

As I dedicated my precious babies to the Lord, it was my greatest desire that they would live a surrendered and committed life to Jesus Christ. I hoped that they and the seed of their generations would carry the good news of the gospel to the ends of the world; that they would be a godly generation; and that they would live a life glorifying Jesus Christ and reaching the world with the wonderful news of salvation (John 3:16).

The Lord blessed me richly with two lovely children and the following year with another beautiful baby boy; Vincent. Truly, what joy as a mother to have three beloved children. What joy!

During these years, however, there were great struggles in my marriage. Sadly, after many years of a very painful marriage, Victor's father left our home for the last time and did not return. We later divorced. The Lord was truly faithful and my provider during these years as He journeyed with me. I sought to instruct my children in the ways of the Lord. He faithfully journeys today with my adult children, grandchildren, and me. What an awesome God we serve!

Victor encountered many doctor and emergency room visits due to asthma and stomach issues, but he remained a sweet and joyful baby, *always smiling*. As an infant, Victor suffered with many painful hernias. After various surgeries, God enabled him to bounce back with strength and joy. The surgeries were very difficult for me as I waited for my son to endure the pre-op and the recovery phases of his surgery. Even now, my heart saddens as I remember the various surgeries my son endured. But God in His faithfulness quickly healed Victor after each surgery, which was a great comfort to me.

God gave Victor a heart of compassion even as a child; he would always tell me of his love for me, and in his own child-like words, he would remind me that Jesus Christ loved me. His tight hugs and wet kisses always brought me great joy. That compassion was directed toward others as well. If he saw someone crying, he would go and hug that person whether it was a child or an adult.

When my children were young, and in later years as well, my career consisted of work as a counselor and as a director of a high-risk prevention / intervention program. In one of the programs that I developed, there was a participant who was greatly struggling and emotionally broken. This program consisted of men and women whose lives and choices had caused emotional pain and a downward spiral of despair. As I sat with the other participants and with Victor under a mother's protective watch, he went and gave the individual who was emotionally broken a warm hug. Later, I received a letter at my office from the individual to whom Victor showed love. This precious individual shared that he was at the point of giving up on life. He felt hopeless and despaired of life, but my son's expression of love encouraged him and gave him hope.

Christmastime brought some of my fondest memories with my children. As a single parent, my heart would always rejoice as I watched God's great provision of gifts and a wonderful meal. On Christmas morning, we would pray and thank the Lord for His wonderful provision. I loved to see my children's eyes light up with excitement and joy as they saw the gifts the Lord had provided. Victor would always kiss and hug me and say thank you. Oh, how my heart misses Victor's kisses and warm hugs! With immense joy, I will one day see my gentle giant again, never to depart (John 3:16).

As a child, Victor was very kind and loved to share with others. When another child hurt him or wounded his heart, my son would always forgive. Victor never held grudges, even as an adult, toward someone who brought offense. As an adult, he would interact with the individual with Christ-like wisdom and love.

At a particular Christian school that Victor was attending, there was a child who was very angry and bullied other students. One day at school he walked up to my son and smacked him. Later that day, Victor discussed the matter with me. I asked him how he was doing as I listened to the hurtful event; I then hugged and kissed him. As I comforted my son, I discussed with Victor in detail the situation concerning the other child.

The next day I went to Victor's school. Victor and I met with the other student and their teacher; the student's face was full of sadness as he communicated with great anger. As the meeting continued, the student asked for Victor's forgiveness. Victor then stood up and walked over to the other child, weeping, as he told the child that he forgave him. This was truly a display of my son's kindness and love that was God's gift to him.

Victor was a typical child who would fall into mischief. As a toddler, Victor had a habit of biting the ears of other children, though I would always immediately intervene. One day a child bit him back and left an awful bruise. After this experience, Victor never bit another child. When he was about five, he thought he would help his big sister manicure her nails, but this was surely a disaster for her. While she was sleeping, Victor quietly used her nail clipper to cut her beautiful nails. When he finished, they were only ragged stumps. I heard my daughter shrieking "Mom!" as she ran in my direction. Later my daughter lovingly forgave Victor and embraced him with kisses; she would often lovingly hold Victor and Vincent in her lap, embracing them with tender care. Years later, we as a family still laugh about Victor the manicurist.

Victor loved to eat anything and everything that was yummy. During meals, Vincent knew to be watchful of Victor because he was quick to sample some or all of his food. I would often hear, "Mom, Victor ate my food!" I would go to the dining room and discuss the matter once again with Victor, and with a big, innocent smile he would say; "I ate Vincent's food, and I am sorry." He would then seek to share the small amount of the remaining food that he had taken from Vincent's plate. After a process of loving discipline, Victor eventually stopped the habit of eating his brother's food. How that boy loved to eat! Truly, Victor was a very loving child, especially toward his brother and sister. He loved to share his toys and favorite candy with them, with other children, and with me. As the years continued, Victor encouraged me in his child-like faith and love for the Lord. What a joy as Victor always hugged me and said, "Mama, I love you." On the day of Victor's accident as he prepared to leave, he hugged me and said, "Mom, I love you!"

On a very busy morning as I was preparing for work, Vincent, my youngest child, came into my room and said to me, "Mama, I want to be saved" (Luke 18:15–17). I immediately stopped what I was doing, sat Vincent in my lap, and shared with him how he could be saved. What a glorious day that was as my son gave his heart to Jesus Christ (Rom. 10:9–10)!

My son's father was now God Almighty, his Heavenly Father (John 3:16)! Shortly afterward, Vincent shared the wonderful news of his salvation with Victor. Then he prayed with Victor, and he too received Jesus Christ as his Lord and Savior. After hearing the wonderful news, I sat Victor in my lap and explained to him about what he had done. Praise God! Victor understood and rejoiced in his new and precious gift of salvation.

As Victor entered school, his greatest challenge became his greatest strength; he struggled with comprehension skills in his studies. He had to study much harder than his siblings who were accelerated in their studies. When his teachers discussed with me their concerns about Victor's struggle, I prayed and continued to work diligently with him. I soon sought a professional tutor to help him. As the months eventually became years, Victor's tutoring became very costly, but God was faithful! The owner of the tutoring business who was wonderful with Victor trained me to help other students. This training helped me to pay for my gentle giant's tutoring costs as I tutored other students on some evenings.

Throughout Victor's life, his love for Jesus Christ Lord was evident from childhood to adulthood until his eternal home-going. His love for Jesus Christ was a great testimony of our Heavenly Father, and this testimony continues through God's wonderful grace in the lives of others today. Oh, what a precious child Victor was! God taught me so very much through his life about the beauty of unconditional love, mercy, patience, and grace. He and my other children are God's wonderful gift of love to me. Throughout Victor's life here on Earth, he proclaimed his salvation and the glorious day that his brother led him to Jesus Christ and how he too received Jesus Christ as his Lord and Savior. Again, throughout Victor's life from childhood to adulthood, "by the grace of God" he lived out his love for Jesus, sharing God's love and salvation to a hurting, lost and dying world.

As a mother, I sought God's wisdom in teaching my children to love the Lord with all their hearts, souls, and minds (Matt. 22:37). I also taught them to love the Lord more than they could ever love me. Yet Victor taught me the continuous beauty of seeking God's wisdom and will for one's life and loving the Lord with all your heart, mind, and soul. Parents, embrace every moment with your children, loving and instructing them in the Word of God. As you embrace and love them, teach them to love the Lord with all of their heart, mind, and soul (Prov. 22:6). Treasure every moment with your child, for time passes quickly.

Chapter 2

ADOLESCENCE

I will come and proclaim your mighty acts, Sovereign LORD; I will proclaim your righteous deeds, yours alone. Since my youth, God, you have taught me, and to this day I declare your marvelous deeds.

—Psalm 71:16–17, niv

I LOVED THE FREEDOM of Victor's love and relationship with Jesus Christ. The Lord was his "Daddy," his Abba Father. Victor knew that God loved him; He learned with child-like faith to rest in the Lord even when he was afraid and felt insecure. By the grace of God, He embraced the truth that he could surely do all things through Jesus Christ that strengthened him (Phil. 4:13).

Though their father was rarely involved in their lives, as a single mother I prayerfully taught my children to pray for their father and love and respect him. Victor hoped that his father would one day be a part of his life. He shared with me the void he felt without his father. Victor often questioned as an adolescent whether his father loved him, and he began to share his wounded emotions and disappointments as he sought to form a relationship with his father through phone calls—but his father remained absent in his life. Victor learned to rest in the sweet assurances of his Heavenly Father's love; surely, he was not without a father's love.

Moreover, God who is faithful sent many Christian men into his life to love, cherish, encourage, teach, and model the Christian life before him; these men were the precious hands and feet of Jesus Christ

Thank you,
    Mr. Clarence Holmes
    Pastor David Hammontree Sr.
    Pastor Wayne Barber
    Pastor Randy Petersen
    Mr. Tyrone Richmond
    Mr. Kenneth Bryant
    Pastor Greg Hand
    Pastor David Hammontree Jr.
    Mr. Greg Bowman

Mr. Larry Frick
Mr. Steve McCary
Mr. West Bowman

Victor was also blessed with many other wonderful Christians who were the hands and feet of Jesus Christ in his life—teaching him the example of following and loving Jesus Christ. Thank You, Lord!

Two months prior to Victor's heavenly home-going, we were spending the day together when I said to Victor, "Let's go and visit your dad." When we arrived, his father informed us that he had been ill. I will never forget the beautiful picture of seeing Victor put his arms around his father and pray for him. And suddenly, within two months, my gentle giant had passed from this life to his eternal home.

How quickly life passes! While you have breath, live for the glory of God. Continually seek to be a godly example to your children by the power of the Holy Spirit. Also, please seek to reach a hurting, lost, and dying world (James 4:14); embrace those without hope with the hope, salvation, and love of Jesus Christ.

> For God so loved the world that he gave his only begotten Son, that whosoever believeth in him should not perish, but have everlasting life.
> —John 3:16

I give God great glory! Countless times in Victor's life I would hear him ask someone,

"Do you know that God loves you?"

Do *you* know that Jesus Christ died for your sin so that you could be saved and spend eternity with Him? Would you like to know how to become a Christian? As Victor would say, "Do you know Jesus Christ as your Lord and Savior?"

- First: God loves you (Rom. 5:8–9).
- Second: All have sinned (Rom. 3:10–12, 23).
- Third: Sin separates us from God (Rom. 6:23).
- Fourth: God desires to be your Heavenly Father and spend eternity with you (Rev. 3:20; John 1:12; 3:16).

You may ask how you can have this relationship with God through Jesus Christ our Lord:

1. Repent of your sin (Acts 3:19).

2. Believe that Jesus Christ died and rose again that you can have eternal life (John 3:16; 15:13).
3. Repent and receive Jesus Christ as your Lord and Savior. Ask Him to come into your heart as Savior (John 1:12; Rom. 3:20).
4. Allow Jesus Christ to rule over your life (Gal. 2:20); He will do amazing things in your life.

Lord Jesus Christ, please forgive me of my sins, save my soul, and give me eternal life. I believe that You died on the cross for my sins and were resurrected again that I may have eternal life. I repent of all my sins. Please Lord Jesus Christ, come into my heart and become Lord of my life. Take total control of my life; I surrender (Gal. 2:20) my life to You. Thank You, Lord Jesus Christ, for Your love in receiving my prayer and saving my soul. In Jesus' name, I pray. Amen.

Victor, my gentle giant, was a very kind and respectful youth. His love for Jesus Christ was shown in his relationships with me, his siblings, and all who knew him. Victor was a giving individual—always seeking to give to those in need, often giving his all.

As an adolescent, Victor loved Jesus Christ and lived a committed life as he sought to surrender every area of his life to Him. Victor made a commitment when he was a teenager to remain a virgin until the Lord sent him a wife. His commitment continued until his eternal home-going. Though shy, Victor would share his commitment with his peers and encourage them to know Jesus Christ as their personal Savior. At times he would encounter mockery, but Victor continued to lovingly share the good news of the gospel with his peers.

I loved to hear Victor pray. His prayers were often of few words, but his love and care were wonderfully shown in his prayers. When someone was hurting or in sorrow, he would quietly sit with them tending to their needs. Victor's obedience was one of great respect to the Lord as he often sought God's wisdom. He and I would prayerful seek the Lord if he was not sure that the decision he was seeking to make was God's plan for his life.

Nonetheless, like any teen, when Victor would make a decision that was not wise, I would lovingly and at times firmly intervene. One of these occasions was after I had purchased a Jeep and asked Vincent and Victor to wash it for me. Victor decided that the chrome hubcaps needed to be white—and that he would surprise me with freshly-painted hubcaps. So Victor used a can of white enamel spray paint that I had in the garage and carefully painted all the chrome hubcaps white.

That I was upset with Victor would be an understatement, but as I began to speak with him about the sprayed hubcaps, I could see godly sorrow as he apologized, acknowledging that he was wrong and that he should have talked with me about the matter first. Victor spent hours removing the paint with cleaners. After hours of scrubbing, Victor came into the house with a big smile and wet, soaked clothes asking me to come out and look at the hubcaps. And, praise God, most of the paint was removed! Victor gave a big sigh of relief and joy.

Though Victor was a quiet individual, he had an enduring strength that was a great encouragement in my life. This enduring strength enabled him to persevere during his journey of life. I often called Victor my gentle giant due to his humble, kind, and loving heart—as well as the strength that I saw in his journey of life. What an awesome God we serve!

From childhood on, every night after my children went to bed, I would kneel beside their beds and pray that God would make them mighty for Him. All three of my children attended wonderful Christian schools. Vincent and Tondra excelled in school, but Victor worked twice as hard, studying late and waking in the early morning. Victor studied by kneeling on the floor and leaning on his bed with his books before him. Victor was a praying student, fervently trusting God that he would pass each course with excellence. Praise God! Though he struggled, Victor would finish each course, greatly glorifying our Heavenly Father.

During the summer, my sons worked at a Christian camp. The camp was on top of a mountain in the area where I live. Because of my fear of driving up the steep roads, prior to that first day of camp, I would always ask, "What is the height of the mountain"? They would laugh as my dread of driving up the mountain continued. As the first journey up the mountain began, we prayed, and the prayers continued with each journey. The camp was on the very top of that mountain. But God!

As the years passed, my heart was blessed as my sons shared with me their adventures. I loved when they would share with me how they ministered God's Word to the camp attendees. Victor loved the yearly special event at the camp that was hosted for special needs children. Oh, how he looked forward to these special events! He would continuously pray for the children as he sought to be the hands and feet of Jesus. I would watch Victor, as a child, tenderly interact with babies and children with special needs; later on as an adult, Victor worked with adults who were mentally challenged. This kind of love was possible only through Jesus our Lord and Savior who loves Victor and died for him. How my heart rejoices over God's great love for Victor as he reigns with Him today.

One year during my children's summer break I did not have the finances to take them on a summer vacation. I decided to take them on an adventurous vacation with discount coupons I had for various hotels, meals, and activities. I packed an ice chest with their favorite snacks and beverages, and we traveled until we found a hotel we all liked. What joy we had together as my children celebrated our adventurous vacation. As we left, Victor said with a big smile, "Mom, thank you." He and my children always were so very thankful, whether they were going to a small restaurant or to Florida.

My gentle giant, from childhood to adolescence, would always say with a big smile, "Mom, thank you for all you do for us." As a man, he never would neglect to say thank you for even the smallest things I did for him. Victor's smile is a beautiful memory I cherish until the blessed day when I will kiss his smiling face.

During school chapel, my youngest son, Vincent, started a ministry in which he and Victor ministered together in music. What joy I felt as I watched my sons minister to other youth in their school. During these wonderful and blessed times, they would sing and share God's Word with fellow classmates. As the years have passed, Vincent became a pastor with a wonderful music ministry that reaches youth and adults around the United States. He ministers the precious gift of salvation and hope.

When he was young, Victor aspired to be a youth pastor. He would often say, "Mom, please pray for me. I really desire to be a youth pastor." Later, Victor excitedly proclaimed, "Mom, I feel God is calling me into ministry!" Though my precious gentle giant did not serve in full-time ministry before his heavenly home-going, he often served with me in ministry, being the hands and feet of Jesus.

At my previous church we would have visitation days. My children and other church members shared the plan of salvation in various communities and homes. How precious it was to see my children give gospel tracts to those we met, telling them in a sweet, shy way about Jesus Christ. How blessed I was as I watched Victor's life and how God used him to plant spiritual seeds in the lives of others... What an awesome God we serve!

One of the things I taught my children was the importance of honesty. Lying was not only wrong; it created distrust in others, and displeased God. As my children became adolescents, I began to often teach them about integrity. One key statement was, "If you lose your integrity, you lose your testimony, your ministry, and the trust of others." I have heard my younger son, Vincent, say this often as an adult. In earlier years, Victor was often very trusting and disappointed by others, but he learned to pray for God's wisdom in his relationships with others. Though he was sometimes disappointed by someone's actions, Victor would allow God's love to enable him to forgive and love them through his disappointment or pain.

Victor was quick to ask for forgiveness if he felt that he had offended someone.

His peers knew that if they shared a private matter with him he would keep it confidential, and Victor prayed for the person who had shared the private matter. Victor also knew that if what was shared was harmful, then he needed to share it with another adult or me. How beautiful are the wonderful memories of my gentle giant. Thank You, Lord.

Victor continued to see avenues open up in school to minister to his peers the hope he had in Jesus Christ. Victor would befriend classmates who were not outgoing and had isolated themselves from their peers. He would talk to them, listening to their goals and aspirations in life, yet always seeking to share salvation with them or encourage a fellow Christian to live for Jesus Christ.

While Victor was often quiet, God's power equipped and gifted him with great wisdom and love. Victor reached those who isolated themselves out of fear and rejection, encouraging them with God's great love and the hope that is found in Him. Victor loved those God-given moments when he was able to share the wonderful good news of the gospel.

Victor, my amazing son, was a beautiful treasure from the Lord. I greatly rejoice in God's faithfulness and love for my gentle giant. God's love and wisdom in my son's life manifested in the sweet assurance Victor had of God's love for a hurting, lost, and dying world. It was his great desire that every man, woman, boy, and girl would spend eternity with our Savior Jesus Christ. This great love of my Heavenly Father also resounds in my heart as I tell a hurting, lost, and dying world that Jesus Christ saves. Praise the Lord, eternity awaits!

Chapter 3

ADULTHOOD

And how shall they preach, except they be sent? as it is written, How beautiful are the feet of them that preach the gospel of peace, and bring glad tidings of good things!
—ROMANS 10:15

Oh, my dear and precious son, how I miss you! Yet, by God's grace, I journey seeking to reach a hurting, lost, and dying world and rejoicing that there will come a day when my life will pass from this life to eternity. My heart rejoices that I will embrace you, my son, again. By God's wonderful and mighty grace, my heart rejoices as I write this chapter as I share the life of my precious gentle giant, Victor Dywon Carr.

Truly, God is faithful beyond measure! How my heart rejoices today as I ponder on my gentle giant's great love for the Lord. Victor greatly loved the Lord, and while he lived here on Earth, he kept journals of his loving and intimate relationship with the Lord. He would often say, "Mom, look what the Lord spoke to my heart." With great excitement, He would wake me up even if I was asleep. These journals will be treasures in my heart until I see my beloved son again.

Victor was a young man of faith (Luke 1:37), embracing each impossible situation and believing that God was able do the impossible. He knew that if God did not answer his prayer, then the Lord's plan was better. Victor believed in praying about matters in his life and seeking the Lord before he moved forward. I was greatly blessed when I observed Victor patiently waiting on the Lord. When the Lord answered, Victor would proclaim God's faithfulness with great joy. Victor's joy was the same whether the Lord answered his desire or had another plan.

When my heart was troubled, my precious son would always comfort me with a hug, prayers, and God's Word. He would comfort me with words like, "Mom, it is going to be alright," and "God will work it out."

One difficult day Victor saw that my heart was troubled. Victor dearly loved me and knew when I was wounded. I often sought to hide it from him because he always tried to protect me. On that particular day Victor was riding with me and asked me to stop at the store. Later, he sat in the car and handed me a cross made out of glass. Inscribed on the cross were these words:

> But Jesus beheld them, and said unto them, With men this is impossible; but with God all things are possible.
> —Matthew 19:26

I hugged my precious son. His gift was to remind me that I could bring every problem, heartache, and trial of life to the cross; nothing was impossible with God.

My son Victor was a precious young man who loved his Lord and Savior with all of his heart, mind, and soul, and my gentle giant lives with Him today. A godly young man of valor, he committed to remain a virgin until he married, and "by the grace of God" he did so until his journey from this life to eternity. Yet, as a virgin prior to his home-going he sought and prayed to the Lord for a wife. As a precious, godly man, he lived and sought to serve the Lord in obedience and commitment in reaching a hurting, lost, and dying world.

He sought never to compromise this obedience and commitment to the Lord his Savior who had placed this in his heart and life. Yet, Victor lovingly sought to share the gospel with family, friends, strangers, and all those he met until his heavenly home-going.

Victor loved his family members dearly. He greatly loved his little brother; Vincent. He would be excited about the work of Jesus Christ in Vincent's life as he reached out to a hurting, lost, and dying world. Throughout his journals, I read his beautiful prayers concerning his brother's ministry and family, and I am blessed. I love reading about his joy when he had opportunities to serve and help Vincent in ministry. Victor greatly loved his big sister too. He lovingly referred to her as his "Sus," and he continually sought to encourage and bless her.

Victor loved his nieces and nephews. He mentored them by God's grace, being salt and light in their lives. Victor took every opportunity to share God's Word with them, and if he did not know the answer to one of their questions, he would research the answer. He would patiently sit with them and teach them God's Word and biblical truth. Victor was a wonderful uncle and loving encouragement in their lives. He would faithfully be involved in their school activities and extracurricular activities. From adolescence to adulthood, Victor enjoyed cooking. He would use whatever ingredients available and make delicious meals. But Victor especially enjoyed cooking and inviting his nieces and nephews and others to his feast. Victor's barbecue and ice cream pies are what my grandchildren enjoyed the most.

On the day of Victor's passing, though he had worked third shift as a program specialist with mentally challenged adults, he got ready to pick up my grandson who needed a ride home from football practice. Shortly after arriving home from work, he prepared to leave and pick him up. I told Victor that he really needed to rest, but being a man of integrity, he stated, "Mom, I gave A.J. my word that I would pick him up."

On the day that my gentle giant passed from this life, he was doing what he greatly loved, encouraging and helping his nieces and nephews. He had planned to spend the day with them, embracing them with God's love. What an awesome God we serve! My oldest grandson had actually given his life to Jesus Christ two days prior to Victor's home-going, for which I give God glory! (John 3:16)

Victor often sought to carry the wonderful good news of the gospel to a hurting, lost, and dying world. He would often share with me the wonderful opportunities he had sharing God's Word with those he met and those he knew. Victor also loved to serve those in full-time ministry by walking beside them, praying and serving along with them. As a full-time missionary, God gave me the wonderful privilege to be one of those Victor served beside.

As a missionary, God continues to open doors and enable me to reach a hurting, lost, and dying world in the United States and internationally. Yearly, the Lord continues to give me direction in reaching communities of single-parent families through a wonderful event called "Celebration of Hope."

This wonderful event enables me and a precious host of volunteers that journey with me yearly to reach single-parent families and communities with the only true hope of salvation. It is a time of great celebration for the love that the Lord has for reaching a hurting, lost, and dying world. Victor would joyfully and tirelessly serve the many families that attended Celebration of Hope. His greatest joy, however, was serving the children, sharing God's Word, love, and wonderful gift of salvation with them.

I truly believe his greatest challenge was serving with me on a missions trip that I organized with a group of wonderful Christians. This was a four-day missions trip in the United States. It was a difficult time, and many rejected Jesus Christ as Lord and Savior. Though Victor was disappointed, he continued to pray for their souls (John 3:16). The individuals in this community angrily rejected God's Word, though none of those who attended sought to condemn that community but to love them and share with them the good news that Jesus Christ greatly loved them and so desired that they would become His children.

As an adult, Victor's desire to be a youth pastor remained until the day of his heavenly home-going. He had planned to take some seminary courses. Victor would always say, "Mom, keep praying concerning my serving as a youth pastor." By God's grace, Victor continued to serve in places of ministry where the Lord called him to serve. Victor continued to seek the Lord in places of ministry until the Lord called him to his eternal home. Victor served with me in ministry, seeking to bless those with whom he came in contact through a kind smile or loving service. Two months prior to Victor's passing, I was planning for the Hope Unlimited Ministry's yearly single-parent Christmas ministry event which Victor was so looking forward to. He loved blessing a child with gifts. Victor was preparing to do what he loved the most and that was helping children.

His greatest desire was to serve the Lord with all his heart and trust Him in his journey of life. I remember those beautiful days as if they were yesterday; how he would rejoice when he had shared Jesus Christ with a hurting, lost, and dying world.

FORGIVENESS

By the grace of God, my precious Victor was a wise adult who continued to show forgiveness and love toward those who were unloving. Victor would forgive freely, releasing the matter to our Lord and Savior Jesus Christ.

Victor was also kind in his response to those who offended him and sought godly wisdom. I often would see Victor later help this individual with various needs he or she may have had. Victor believed that when these situations occurred God would surely settle the matter and use it for His glory. God used this wisdom in Victor's life to bless my life as he would often say, "Mom, pray and seek God about the situation." Victor's strength, love, and patience taught me priceless lessons that I will forever embrace in life until the appointed day when I will see Victor and my Lord and Savior face to face.

Victor cherished close friendships with other Christians and the support and prayers that they provided. The Lord blessed Victor with many precious folks who loved him. Victor loved people and listened to their journeys and the troubles of their hearts. As he would often say to me, "Mom, I am praying for this or that person"—or he would ask me to pray for them without disclosing their private matter. Often he prayed for a co-worker or resident where he worked. Victor did not criticize people, but with great concern ask me to pray for a troubled individual or one who did not know Jesus Christ as their Lord and Savior.

One day after returning from work he shared with me that a co-worker had used harsh words toward him, including profanity, because that employee felt that he was too religious. After we discussed the matter, I shared with him that I felt that he needed to discuss this matter with administration. He gently stated, "Mom, I am going to let God handle this matter." Later, after Victor's home-going, this employee gave their life to Jesus Christ. Victor's heart and love for the lost and for the backslidden was lost even until his life passed from this life to eternity. Yet, his

Adulthood

love continued for the lost and Christian believers who were backslidden and away from the Lord until his home-going. Praise the Lord!

Victor greatly loved God's Word, but he had a passion for reading and learning about the Book of Revelation. He loved sermons, CDs, books, and teaching on the Book of Revelation; he was always excited to hear biblical truths about the Book of Revelation. I felt that the study of Revelation was truly an in-depth study, but Victor loved quoting things he had learned about the Book of Revelation. I truly believe that Victor's heart at times longed and yearned for heaven as this quotation from one of his journals attests:

> *Dear God, You are someone that I can go to when I am sad or happy or have something on my mind. You are God and will always be there for me. I am Your son Victor; the one You love. I am the one who would do anything for You; if You told me to go, then I will go; if You told me to stay, then I will stay; if You told me to not worry about things of this world, I won't. If You said wait; I will wait (John 3:16).*

When I read Victor's writings, I am so blessed because they resound with his love for the Lord. I am so very thankful that, by God's grace, he lived to be salt and light to those he met. Victor talked often about heaven, the biblical truths that he learned in the Book of Revelation, and what awaited those who know Jesus Christ as Lord and Savior. I will forever remember my gentle giant's words to those with whom he would share God's good news of salvation:

"Do you know that God loves you?"

"Do you know that Jesus Christ died for your sin so that you could be saved and spend eternity with Him?"

"Would you like to know how to become a Christian?"

Victor would share salvation in a simple way to make sure that the listener would understand. How Victor loved people! He prayed that they would be saved and have an intimate relationship with Jesus Christ.

God's enduring grace embraced Victor's life and heart. Victor's love and faith in the Lord is a testimony in my heart; his life reminds me to press on, for the best is yet to come. How I miss my son's loving hugs and kisses on his bearded face. I will forever remember his precious, loving, and profound words, "Mom, I love you!"

Though my life will never be the same without my gentle giant, God's sustaining power holds me gently and at times carries me. He alone enables me to run the race with sweet endurance (Phil. 3:14). And with God's great strength I run. *Praise the Lord!*

As I read Victor's journals they display such a sweet intimate relationship with our Heavenly Father. His journals are like peering into a conversation between a Father and son. How I praise the Lord for the beautiful gifts of Victor's journals! Until I pass from this life to my glorious eternal home, my heart will rejoice because of Victor's love for our Heavenly Father.

Eternity Awaits

Victor enjoyed retreats and the times of biblical teaching and fellowship that they provided. The Lord in his faithfulness mightily used a ministry retreat that blessed and greatly encouraged his life. This retreat took place in the mountains for a weekend of biblical teaching and a wonderful time of prayer.

After the retreat ended, relatives of the retreat participants were asked to come to a service that would further bless and encourage the participants. As we stood in the loft the day of service, Victor and the other participants could not see us. Suddenly the lights were turned on. How my heart was blessed when I saw Victor; he had a big, handsome smile on his face when he saw me.

This memory remains in my heart today. Later, I too went on this Christian retreat that women from various communities attended, and on the day of the encouraging service there was my gentle giant with the same big, handsome smile. But this time my son was waving.

I think of heaven when I think of this precious day; when my life passes to my eternal home, I believe Victor will be there waiting with a big, handsome smile saying, "Mom, you are finally home." And I will hold and kiss him with a million kisses.

I will see my Heavenly Father and embrace Him for what may seem a million years. What a day of great rejoicing that will be!

> For God so loved the world, that he gave his only begotten Son, that whosoever believeth in him should not perish, but have everlasting life.
> —John 3:16

Suddenly: The Years Have Passed

> Why, you do not even know what will happen tomorrow. What is your life? You are a mist that appears for a little while and then vanishes.
> —James 4:14, NIV

Without notice, my life changed on October 11, 2010. The years have passed since my gentle giant passed from this life to eternity with our Heavenly Father. I continue to rejoice that God has been faithful; I have surely seen His goodness in the land of the living (Ps. 23:6). Whether in the times of missing my gentle giant and desiring to embrace him with a mother's kiss, or in the journey of life, God never fails; He forever remains faithful.

The seasons in our lives that arise suddenly do not take our Heavenly Father by surprise because He is God and He knows our tomorrows. Praise God! The years have passed, and His work of ministry continues in my life in reaching a hurting, lost, and dying world. Though at times I long to kiss the face of my son, my greatest desire is to be a vessel of salt and light (Matt. 5:11–17). God is truly faithful beyond measure in the season of sorrow, longing, and pain. As your healer, peace, and strength, He will journey with you through life's seasons as your healer and your Abba Father. Embrace the Lord, for He is your shelter in the storms of life and in your season of healing. The Lord will forever journey with you, for He never lets His children journey alone in their sorrow.

Study Guide

The following chapters are a study guide. Each page reflects my story and God's healing in the journey of grief that He faithfully provides for His children. Through the study guide, you will find various comments repeated on occasion such as, "You never journey alone," "God carries us in our grief," and others. I pray that these statements will resound with gentle grace and truth in your heart and greatly encourage you in your journey of grief.

Chapter 4

SORROW

God, Our Comfort in Our Sorrow

The LORD is my shepherd; I shall not want. He maketh me to lie down in green pastures: he leadeth me beside the still waters. He restoreth my soul: he leadeth me in the paths of righteousness for his name's sake. Yea, though I walk through the valley of the shadow of death, I will fear no evil: for thou art with me; thy rod and thy staff they comfort me. Thou preparest a table before me in the presence of mine enemies: thou anointest my head with oil; my cup runneth over. Surely goodness and mercy shall follow me all the days of my life: and I will dwell in the house of the LORD forever.
—Psalm 23

After Victor's home-going to his heavenly home, my heart longed for his presence. Yet the Lord sustained me in my sorrow and held me tightly in the presence of His awesome and powerful love. Though I would weep for Victor's loving arms and words, God's Word would continually reminded me that I would see my gentle giant again. I remember one day coming home and receiving a blanket from my son Vincent's precious mother-in-law. As I opened the beautiful blanket and read the writing, I began to weep loudly, longing for my baby. At that very moment, the Lord's presence embraced me and held me close as the tears of sorrow became my platform of God's awesome and powerful peace. Truly, what an awesome God we serve!

Sorrow in the home-going of a loved one is not easily defined. In my sorrow I felt that I was in a battle; the overwhelming reality of Victor's home-going threatened to overwhelm me. But God! His presence stood firm in the midst of these emotions, and He held me until the storm of sorrows passed over me.

God's presence prevailed and enabled me to live. Yes, I have life in spite of the sorrow and pain of my son's passing. And by His grace, the Lord continues to help me to press on (Phil. 4:13) and live out His plans and purpose for my life (Luke 1:37). The Lord in His faithfulness would never allow the sorrows of grief to become a tidal wave of defeat and total despair (Isa. 43:2). God's immeasurable grace, strength, and love steadfastly anchors us.

Dear Lord,

Please hold me close as the storms of sorrow pass over. Lord God, though my heart yearns at times to hold and embrace my Victor once again, You give me sweet assurance that I will see my beloved one again.

Thank You, Lord, that Your children are never alone; You are our strength and stronghold.

God knows our sorrows (Heb. 4:14–16); He sent His only son to die for the sins of every man, woman, boy, and girl. His mercy and great compassion comforts us in our sorrow and pain. God never leaves His children alone (Heb. 13:5). There will come a day when your broken heart will heal, your tears will begin to cease, and surely joy will come again. This season of sorrow will surely pass.

I define *sorrow* as a regret or heartache because of the loss of a loved one, a defeating or devastating situation, or a loss in one's life.

▶ Are you struggling in your sorrow of grief? Please explain:

_____

_____

_____

▶ Has your journey of sorrow been one of days, months, or years? Please explain:

_____

_____

_____

▶ Are you *embracing God's healing* in your journey of sorrow, or are you only *embracing the journey of sorrow?* Please explain:

_____

_____

_____

God is faithful! His love for you will never change.
God Almighty…

- Loves you (John 3:16)
- Has compassion for you (Ps. 116:5)
- Has a plan for your life (Jer. 29:11–14)
- Will seek to journey with you (Ps. 55:22)
- Will never leave nor forsake you (Heb. 13:5)
- Gives you hope (Ps. 71:14)
- Sees your tears (Ps. 30:5)
- Sees your broken heart (Ps. 34:17–18)
- Sees your emotional pain (Ps. 33:22; 143:8)
- Shelters you (Ps. 32:7)

▶ Is God using your journey of grief as a beautiful means to encourage another in their sorrow? If so, how?

_____

_____

_____

> This I recall to my mind, therefore have I hope. It is of the Lord's mercies that we are not consumed, because his compassions fail not. They are new every morning: great is thy faithfulness. The Lord is my portion, saith my soul; therefore will I hope in him.
> —Lamentations 3:21–24

SORROW

In life's journey we develop our own personal stories as a masterpiece of God's faithfulness. As we heal, God can heal our sorrows and cause us to be a blessed encouragement for others in the journey of sorrow.

▶ Please write out your story of your journey of grief:

_____

_____

_____

► *Though we may have sorrow, God will forever be with us as He heals us in our sorrow.* In reviewing your journey of grief, how have you seen God's faithfulness?

► *The Lord never leaves us to journey alone.* In reviewing your journey of grief, how have you seen God's faithfulness in sending others to comfort you?

► *In our journey of grief, God sustains us moment by moment, day by day.* In reviewing your journey of grief, how have you seen God's faithfulness every day?

▶ Please write five scriptures that *have encouraged* you in your journey of sorrow:

1. _____
2. _____
3. _____
4. _____
5. _____

▶ Please write five scriptures that give you *hope* in your journey of sorrow:

1. _____
2. _____
3. _____
4. _____
5. _____

▶ Please write five scriptures that give you *joy* in your journey of sorrow:

1. _____
2. _____
3. _____
4. _____
5. _____

Please write five biblical characters who experienced God's faithfulness in their lives during great times of trial and heartache.

Here is an example to get you started:

Biblical character: Elijah

God's faithfulness: God's assuring presence, provision, and great faithfulness in a time of overwhelming hopelessness in Elijah's life.

1. Biblical character:

   _____

   God's faithfulness:

   _____

2. Biblical character:

   _____

   God's faithfulness:

   _____

3. Biblical character:

   _____

   God's faithfulness:

   _____

4. Biblical character:

   _____

   God's faithfulness:

   _____

5. Biblical character:

   _____

God's faithfulness:

___

▶ How does God's faithfulness in your life strengthen you in your sorrow? (Lam. 3:21–24)

___

___

___

▶ Are you struggling in your sorrow to believe that joy will ever come again in your life? Please explain:

___

___

___

As shared in earlier chapters, many grieve differently in their journey of grief. Please know that God understands your sorrow and pain. God will not leave you alone in your sorrow and grief. God loves you, understands you and your journey of grief, and will bring you through to a place of healing and hope.

If your tears continuously flow and never seem to stop, please know that God is a healer of broken hearts (Ps. 34:18) and a healer of grief (Isa. 53:5)

Please, know that:

- You are not alone (Heb. 13:5)
- You are not forsaken or abandoned (Isa. 41:10)
- You are loved and not rejected (Jer. 3:3)
- You are not hopeless (Jer. 29:11; Ps. 31:24; 71:14)

God loves you and will surround you with His matchless love. You are greatly loved and never forsaken because God never leaves His children alone. *Never!* While some may define sorrow in a different manner, most of us can agree that when we are in sorrow, we have grief in our core, in the depths of our heart.

Yet, God who is faithful knows our hearts, and He is able to heal the very depths of our grief, sustaining our hearts, minds, and emotions as we journey in our healing.

As we rest in Him, the tidal waves of sorrow will not destroy us, but we will find that God is truly our anchor. His loving grace, strength, and love will be our shield until the storms of sorrow passes over (Ps.115:11; 119:114).

One day your tears will cease, and joy, peace, and hope will resound in your heart. God's hope reigns in the midst of sorrow. Until that appointed time, hold tightly to God's *love* and *His faithful presence* as He brings you through your journey safely to the other side of healing.

> Dear Heavenly Father,
> In the pain of sorrow, Your love prevails with strength and comfort. Thank You, Lord God. You are the healer of wounded emotions, and You rescue us in our pain. I love You, most awesome God.

Chapter 5

DENIAL

Lord, Embrace Me in the Reality of My Sorrow

And as it is appointed unto men once to die, but after this the judgment.
—Hebrews 9:27

Sometimes life changes suddenly, without a moment's notice. For me, a journey unlike any other began, and all I could do was cling to God's strength and awesome love. I knew that I was not alone in this journey that would change my life forever because I knew that the Lord would hold me close. God's children never journey alone (Heb. 13:5b).

When I received the call that my son and grandchildren were in a car accident, I thought that it surely was a minor accident. But when I arrived at the scene of the accident, to my dismay and shock, I found that a mother's greatest fear had become my reality: my son had passed from this life to eternal life.

There were fire trucks and ambulances in the midst of a horrific scene. As I walked toward the car to pray for my son, I saw a tall man standing with his arms folded across his chest next to Victor's car. He stood as though he was waiting on someone; I had never met him before, but as I approached him, he said, "Your son has passed from this life; now go help those in the land of the living." As I turned, I saw the reality of the accident and what was before me.

In spite of what was told me concerning Victor, I began to plead with the Lord to give Victor breath, to give him life again. I prayed and waited, hoping to hear that my precious son had been revived and that he was alive. I prayed to no avail; God's appointed time had become my son's reality. In the midst of my denial, God became my sustainer and greatly assured my heart that I would see my gentle giant again. God understood my sorrow because He had sent His only begotten Son to die for the sin of every man, woman, boy, and girl.

Dear Precious Lord,
Though my heart sought to deny the reality that Victor had passed from this life to eternity, Your love surrounded me as You strengthened me in my

grief. Thank You, Lord. In my tears and pain, You carried me as Your love healed me in my journey of grief. Thank You, Lord for loving Your children beyond measure!

Thank You, Holy Spirit; we are never alone.

> Let your conversation be without covetousness; and be content with such things as ye have: for he hath said, I will never leave thee, nor forsake thee.
> —Hebrews 13:5

Denial is a disbelief in the reality of a situation or of circumstances that have taken place in our lives.

- ▶ Are you struggling to believe that God loves you and cares about your pain? Please explain:

_____

_____

_____

- ▶ Did you earnestly pray in hopes that God would miraculously intervene on behalf of your loved one and the circumstance would change? Please explain:

_____

_____

_____

- ▶ Are you presently or have you in the past struggled with a disarray of painful emotions since the passing of a loved one? Please explain:

_____

_____

_____

- ▶ Did you struggle with overwhelming emotions when you received the news of the passing of your loved one? Please explain:

_____

- ▶ How did you see the Lord minister to you in the midst of these emotions?

- ▶ Did you journey in denial? Please describe the emotional pain of this struggle:

- ▶ If denial has been an issue, how did it prolong your struggle toward emotional healing?

- ▶ Are you presently struggling with the emotions of denial regarding your loved one's passing? Please explain:

- ▶ How has the Lord enabled you to journey through the valley of denial? (The valley of denial is the refusal to accept the reality of the passing of a loved one and prayerfully move forward one day at a time.) Please explain:

▶ If you are still in the valley of denial, are you seeking to trust the Lord and prayerfully move on one day at a time? Please explain:

Though the reality and pain of the passing of your loved one may be great, it is not greater than the love of our Heavenly Father. When one passes through the process of the journey of grief, the Lord gently holds us tightly as we pass through the storm. The Dutch author and speaker Corrie ten Boom often quoted one of her sister Betsie's favorite sayings, "There is no pit so deep that He [God] is not deeper still."[1] You need to know that this is true of your pain as well: there is no pain so deep that God is not deeper still. God will tenderly strengthen and enable you to move forth in the process of healing. God loves you greatly, and you do not journey alone (Isa. 43:2).

Steps to Healing as You Journey out of the Valley of Denial

The journey of grief is a process of healing in which we trust Jesus Christ as our healer (Ps. 34:1–22). He will heal our wounded emotions. Jesus Christ will also heal our sorrow in the depths and core of our pain. Though we each may grieve differently, the Lord will embrace us in our pain and journey with us in our grief.

You are never alone (Heb. 13:5), for Jesus Christ will never leave or forsake us. Let's review these steps below:

- Cry out to the Lord (2 Sam. 22:6–7)
- Grieve: Jesus will journey with you in your grief (Ps. 29:11)
- Seek the Lord through prayer and His Word (2 Sam. 22:31; Prov. 30:5; Phil. 4:6)

---

1 http://en.wikipedia.org/wiki/Corrie_ten_Boom

- Pour out your heart to the Lord with every emotional pain, fear, struggle, and despair.
- Ask God to heal you in your journey of grief and give you strength and grace to accept the homecoming of your loved one (Ps. 147:3).
- Trust God with all your heart, and *surely* He will see you through; life will again have meaning. (Prov. 3:5–6)

The struggle with denial delays the healing process that every heart must journey through. We may fear a total emotional breakdown or the possibility that despair will cause us to give up on life. Yet God is able! (Rom. 4:20–21) He will embrace you and carry you through these turbulent times.

Do not despair or give up; Jesus Christ too endured the painful encounters of life and understands your pain. He endured death on the Cross so that we would have eternal life—and praise the Lord! He rose again. For every believer, death is not final because Jesus Christ defeated death on the Cross. And surely every individual who has truly received Jesus Christ as Lord and Savior has received eternal life.

(Excerpt: *My Journey Home: There is Hope for Single-Parent Families and Hurting Women*)

> For God so loved the world that he gave his one and only Son, that whoever believes in him shall not perish but have eternal life.
> —John 3:16, niv

God understands your pain because of His great love for every man, woman, boy, and girl. He provided a remedy for sin through the shed blood of Jesus Christ, His only begotten Son. When Jesus Christ died on the Cross, you were on His mind. God loves you with a love that far exceeds the comprehension of the human mind. Jesus endured death on the Cross, yet rose again so that we might be saved and have eternal life. Hallelujah!

> "Where, O death, is your victory? Where, O death, is your sting?" The sting of death is sin, and the power of sin is the law. But thanks be to God! He gives us the victory through our Lord Jesus Christ.
> —1 Corinthians 15:55–57, niv

Remember, you are not alone; the Lord will see you through, dear one. Your emotions of grief, pain, emptiness, and even despair will not consume you. You will heal, and life will once again have meaning as you trust and seek your Heavenly Father who heals us in our grief.

God loves you and desires to be your friend and constant companion. But if you do not know Jesus Christ as your personal Lord and Savior, today is the day to receive Him. Truly Jesus Christ loves you and desires to spend eternity with you.

(Excerpt: *My Journey Home: Jesus Christ the Rescuer of Wounded Emotions*)

Do you know Jesus Christ as your personal Lord and Savior? Jesus Christ will forever love and pursue individuals that they may be saved and birthed into the kingdom of God. You may ask, "How do I become a Christian and be birthed into the kingdom of God?"

- First: God loves you (Rom. 5:8–9)
- Second: All have sinned (Rom. 3:10–12, 23).
- Third: Sin separates us from God (Rom. 6:23).
- Fourth: God desires to be your Heavenly Father and spend eternity with you (Rev. 3:20; John 1:12; 3:16).

You may ask how you can have this relationship with God through Jesus Christ our Lord:

1. Repent of your sin (Acts 3:19).
2. Believe that Jesus Christ died and rose again that you can have eternal life (John 3:16; 15:13).
3. Repent and receive Jesus Christ as your Lord and Savior. Ask Him to come into your heart as Savior (John 1:12; Rom. 3:20).
4. Allow Jesus Christ to rule over your life (Gal. 2:20); He will do amazing things in your life.

Lord Jesus Christ, please forgive me of my sins, save my soul, and give me eternal life. I believe that You died on the cross for my sins and were resurrected again that I may have eternal life. I repent of all my sins. Please, Lord Jesus Christ, come into my heart and become Lord of my life. Take total control of my life; I surrender (Gal. 2:20) my life to You. Thank You, Lord Jesus Christ, for Your love in receiving my prayer and saving my soul. In Jesus' name, I pray. Amen.

If you have truly received Jesus Christ as your Lord and Savior, your life will never be the same. As a daughter of my Heavenly Father, my life has changed forever. He embraced and carried me through my journey of healing when my gentle giant passed from this life to eternity.

If you have chosen to live your life without Jesus Christ, please know that my Heavenly Father will forever love you though you have chosen eternity without Him (John 3:16). Jesus greatly loves you and desires to be your Lord and Savior.

The journey of personal grief is a path that you never need to walk alone. God's love seeks to hold and carry you through your tears and longing. As you seek Him, you will be strengthened as you journey with Him.

Though your journey may differ from another's, one day you will smile again as you trust the Lord and His wonderful grace. I praise the Lord that I can now laugh again and rejoice as God continues to be my sustaining hope. He continuously gives me peace in the midst of my journey.

You will smile again, and surely life will have greater meaning…rejoice! Remember God never lets His children journey alone. God loves you beyond measure; His mercy and love is toward every man, woman, boy, and girl.

> This I recall to my mind, therefore I have hope. Through the Lord's mercies we are not consumed, because His compassions fail not. They are new every morning; great *is* Your faithfulness. "The Lord *is* my portion," says my soul, "Therefore I hope in Him!"
>
> —LAMENTATIONS 3:21–24, NKJV

Dear Heavenly Father,

Truly, You are a faithful Father. Thank You, Lord, for giving me hope and peace when life does not make sense. Thank You, Lord, for healing my wounded emotions and broken heart as You faithfully loved me in my pain and journey of healing. Thank You, precious Heavenly Father, that in our pain, tears, and sorrow You gently embrace us with Your love and hold us close to Your loving heart (Psalm 34:1–22).

Chapter 6

ANGUISH

Lord, Heal My Wounded Emotions

This I recall to my mind, therefore have I hope. It is of the Lord's mercies that we are not consumed, because his compassions fail not. They are new every morning: great is thy faithfulness.

—Lamentations 3:21–23

After a glorious day celebrating the home-going of my precious son with a wonderful police escort in honor of Victor, we headed to the cemetery. Pastor Hammontree blessed us with words of encouragement and hope in the great reunion to come as my children and I had three doves released above the area of my son's burial site.

As we were preparing to leave, the workmen began lowering Victor's body into the ground. Suddenly there began a grip in my heart that only a mother can understand. I immediately asked the director of the cemetery if the workmen would please wait until we left. As the funeral car journeyed to take us home, how the emotions of my heart cried out, "Lord, help me!" For a moment my fleshly emotion cried out, "Oh no! This is final." But a greater power stood up in me with a shout, "It is not final. Victor lives today!" Suddenly the overwhelming emotions left, and the Lord's peace greatly reigned in my heart. Oh, what a glorious moment! While in the depths of overwhelming emotions, God Almighty rescued me! He rescued me and held me close in His peace that has sustained me until this day. He holds me and surrounds me with songs of rejoicing (Zeph. 3:17).

As we continued to journey home, the Lord gave me a promise that though Victor was now with Him, His peace would mightily abide in my home, and He would forever be my protection. Because of Jesus Christ, today I stand.

Dear Abba Father, Daddy,

Thank You for Your love. In the midst of my anguish, You alone rescued me. Lord, You took my emotions of sorrow and anguish and set me free. Thank You, Lord, for strengthening me with comfort beyond measure!

I love You, my Abba Father. Thank You for never allowing Your children to journey alone as they seek and trust You (Zeph. 3:17).

Questions

Often the emotions of anguish leave one in a state of despair and defeat. The pain of anguish for someone who is grieving is real and can be overwhelming.

- ▶ Are you struggling with anguish? How has this affected you in your journey of grief? (Anguish relates to a heartfelt struggle of pain, grief, or sorrow.)
  Please explain:

  _____
  _____
  _____

- ▶ Do you feel alone in your emotion of anguish? If so, please explain:

  _____
  _____
  _____

- ▶ If you are struggling with anguish, do you struggle with hopelessness? If so, please explain:

  _____
  _____
  _____

- ▶ Do you feel despairing of life like one living in a downward spiral of despair? If, so please explain:

  _____

As you journey in your emotions of anguish, please prayerfully share these emotions with a friend, pastor, and / or professional biblically-based counselor.

Many have asked about the pain of my anguish. My response is that in the depths of my anguish and longing God met me. Through the tears and sorrow, God was my anchor of peace and hope that sustained me and strengthened me in my journey of grief—and He sustains me today! The Lord comforted me in my grief and sorrow. Though my gentle giant Victor has passed from this life, God reminded me that surely I will see him again (John 3:16).

Let me repeat, when someone is struggling with anguish, these emotions may lead to a downward spiral of despair and hopelessness. The pain of anguish for one in grief is real, but God is the healer and delivers us in our anguish and wounded emotions.

When struggling with the emotion of anguish, please:

1. Pray and seek the Lord (Prov. 3:5).
2. Acknowledge your anguish before Abba Father, Daddy (Heb. 4:16).
3. Do not deny the emotions that you are feeling (1 Pet. 5:6–7).

Again, share with a friend, pastor, or counselor how each emotion causes you to feel. If you are unable to express your emotions, please consider writing them down on paper. Give yourself time to express the emotions that you may be feeling. If you are unable to express these emotions and are having increasing depression and overwhelming emotions, please consider a counselor. (At times, there are those in this journey who may need the intervention of counseling from a professional biblically-based counselor.) By God's grace, if you are presently on a journey of healing, press on! Your healing will come; your weeping will cease; and joy will come in the morning (Ps. 30:5b).

My blessed hope is that my earthly goodbye was not final because I will see my gentle giant again. God loves you greatly and is the healer of all wounded emotions. Only Jesus Christ is able to heal the wounded heart and the mind that is burdened with grief. Jesus Christ will enable you, one day at a time, to heal in the midst of your anguish. Each day will bring strength in your pain and grief. God will hold, heal, and sustain you until the emotions of grief pass over.

Dear one, God will not leave you alone. He will surely meet you at your point of grief and pain. You are not alone; *no*, never alone! God will surely be your strength and stronghold. He will hold you in the turbulent times of life. God will *not* fail you.

> *Oh Lord, in the midst of my anguish and pain, You rescued me. Thank You, Lord, for Your awesome faithfulness that shelters, protects, and keeps us in the midst of the storm. Thank You Lord, for Your peace that passes all understanding... Thank You, Lord!*

Chapter 7

SADNESS

Lord, You Are My Hope in My Saddened Heart

To console those who mourn in Zion, to give them beauty for ashes, the oil of joy for mourning, the garment of praise for the spirit of heaviness; that they may be called trees of righteousness, the planting of the LORD, that He may be glorified.

—Isaiah 61:3, nkjv

My son Victor lived with me until his eternal journey with the Lord. Though I rejoice that my son knows the Lord as His personal Redeemer and Savior; yet I long at times to kiss his cheeks and embrace his big, burly frame. There are times that I so long for him to enter the door with his famous words, "What's up, Mama?" as I smiled and my heart rejoiced to see him. When these days come, the Lord comforts me in my longing and lovingly reminds me that I will see my gentle giant again. Through Jesus Christ, the sorrow of death does not quench the sustaining hope that Christian believers have in Him.

I have truly found that in the moments, days, or weeks when my heart cries out to see Victor, hold him close, and never let him go, God is greater. He is my faithful sustainer even in my tears (Ps. 30:5b) Also, I have found that God is greater than the depths of a grieving heart. So until I see my precious son again and meet my Lord face to face, I will continue to press in and press on, embracing His plans and purposes for my life.

> *Dear Heavenly Father,*
> *Thank You for hearing the cry of Your children and comforting us in our sorrow. Thank You, faithful Heavenly Father and companion; in the depths of our emotions, You comfort us and never forsake us.*

Sadness for many includes a yearning to once again embrace the presence of a loved one who has passed from this life. Sadness is an emotion of grief which may be overwhelming; you may feel lonely and isolated. But *Elohim,* our loving and merciful Heavenly Father, never leaves His children alone. He is also merciful, loving, and compassionate to those who do not know His Son Jesus Christ as the Messiah.

> For God so loved the world that He gave His only begotten Son, that whoever believes in Him should not perish but have everlasting life.
> —John 3:16, NKJV

Our Heavenly Father knows our tears and sorrow (Ps. 30:5b). You are not alone! God's Word states,

> Seeing then that we have a great high priest, that is passed into the heavens, Jesus the Son of God, let us hold fast our profession. For we have not an high priest which cannot be touched with the feeling of our infirmities; but was in all points tempted like as we are, yet without sin. Let us therefore come boldly unto the throne of grace, that we may obtain mercy, and find grace to help in time of need.
> —Hebrew 4:14–16

God states in His Word that He hears our cries; He sees the sadness that touches the hearts of those in sorrow. God sees and know all things; He truly cares for and loves you. Some of these promises are illustrated in the following verses:

- Jeremiah 23:23–24; Psalm 44:21; Psalm 139:1–18; Proverbs 15:3
- Isaiah 41:10; 1 John 3:20; Hebrews 13:5; Hebrews 4:13–16
- John 21:15–17; Psalm 147:5; Genesis 16:13; Romans 11:36
- Psalm 147; Isaiah 55:8–9; Psalm 62:1–2; 1 John 3:19–20
- Matthew 10:29–30; Isaiah 43; Psalm 91:11–14; John 10:14
- Zephaniah 3:17; Jeremiah 31:3; Isaiah 44:24; Jeremiah 29:11–13
- Psalm 46:10; Lamentations 3:21–24; Deuteronomy 31:6; Psalm 37:25
- Psalm 9:18; Psalm 25:5; Psalm 33:20; Psalm 38:15

Sadness, for many, may feel like being encircled in a wall of hopelessness. Overwhelming emotions can stagnate the healing process; the walls of hopelessness can become a hiding place for wounded emotions. The journey of grief is not without sorrow and tears, yet God is able to heal the deep wound of sadness and despair. These emotions may be due to the yearning for a loved one and the pain of the void that their passing has left in our heart. Yet, there is a struggle to move forward. As we surrender our struggles to the Lord, He will enable us to journey in our healing one day at a time. Our healing is not defined by the process of another's healing, but by God's mercy, grace, and love. The Lord embraces His children and meets them at their point of need and pain; we are never alone, never alone. Remember, there is no pain so deep that God's love and healing is not deeper still.

Dear Precious Savior,

Though many hearts have struggled in the journey of healing, I praise and thank You that we have never journeyed alone. Your mighty presence and steadfast love have been our strength and hope. Thank You, Lord Jesus Christ, for never letting Your children journey alone.

▸ Please describe your personal journey of sadness:

_____

_____

_____

▸ Are you presently struggling with the passing of a loved one? If yes, please explain:

_____

_____

_____

▸ What are these struggles?

_____

_____

_____

- What are you embracing and not willing to surrender to Jesus Christ in your journey of sadness?

_____
_____
_____

- How has it affected you to embrace these struggles and not allow the Lord to heal you?

_____
_____
_____

- What have you had to surrender to the Lord in this journey?

_____
_____
_____

- How have you seen the Lord journey with you in your sadness? Please explain:

_____
_____
_____

…weeping may endure for a night, but joy cometh in the morning.
—Psalm 30:5b

- Please describe what this scripture means to you.

_____
_____
_____

Sadness

- Will you surrender your struggle(s) to the Lord today so you can be set free? Please write a prayer of release, if so.

_____
_____
_____
_____

- Do you personally believe that your grief is greater than God? If yes, please describe:

_____
_____
_____

> You are of God, little children, and have overcome them, because He who is in you is greater than he who is in the world.
> —1 John 4:4, nkjv

- Please describe what "greater is He that is within me" means to you:

_____
_____
_____

- Is God greater than our *weaknesses?* (2 Cor. 12:9)

_____
_____
_____

- Is God greater than our *fears?* (Ps. 34:4)

_____
_____

- Is God greater than our *loneliness?* (Heb. 13:5)

- Is God greater than our *brokenheartedness?* (Ps. 34:4)

- Is God greater than our *wounded emotions?* (Ps. 34:18)

- Is there anything impossible with God? (Mark 10:27; Luke 1:37)

- Is God able to restore your joy? (Ps. 30:5b)

  Yes

  No

Do you truly believe that one day your joy will come again? I can truly say with a resounding "Yes!" that as you trust the Lord, though your faith may seem as small as a mustard seed (Luke 17:5–6), God will provide the strength, joy, and hope that you need in your journey of grief (Ps. 30:5b).

Remember: though your journey of healing may differ from another's, your joy will surely come in the morning. With God's healing and joy beyond measure in my heart, I proclaim God's goodness and faithfulness: He will not fail you or forsake you. You are greatly loved, and God never leaves His children alone. He is merciful, loving, and compassionate toward those who do not know His Son as Lord and Savior. God's love is beyond our comprehension and comparison.

His love surpasses any human love that you may receive. God does not stop loving you—because His love is not conditional or based on personal performance. Because of His great and mighty love; He sent the gift of His Son; Jesus Christ, who is the Savior of the world. Jesus Christ died for every man, woman, boy, and girl.

He is Jesus Christ the Messiah; the Redeemer of the world who truly saves the souls of those who receive Him as Lord and Savior. Yet, for Jesus Christ to become your Redeemer and Lord and Savior, you must be saved.

(Excerpt: *My Journey Home: Jesus Christ the Rescuer of Wounded Emotions*)

Please remember!

- First: God loves you (Rom. 5:8–9).
- Second: All have sinned (Rom. 3:10–12, 23).
- Third: Sin separates us from God (Rom. 6:23).
- Fourth: God desires to be your Heavenly Father and spend eternity with you (Rev. 3:20; John 1:12; 3:16).

You may ask how you can have this relationship with God through Jesus Christ our Lord:

1. Repent of your sin (Acts 3:19).
2. Believe that Jesus Christ died and rose again that you can have eternal life (John 3:16; 15:13).

3. Repent and receive Jesus Christ as your Lord and Savior. Ask Him to come into your heart as Savior (John 1:12; Rom. 3:20).

4. Allow Jesus Christ to rule over your life (Gal. 2:20); He will do amazing things in your life.

Lord Jesus Christ, please forgive me of my sins, save my soul, and give me eternal life. I believe that You died on the cross for my sins and were resurrected again that I may have eternal life. I repent of all my sins. Please Lord Jesus Christ, come into my heart and become Lord of my life. Take total control of my life; I surrender (Gal. 2:20) my life to You. Thank You, Lord Jesus Christ, for Your love in receiving my prayer and saving my soul. In Jesus' name, I pray. Amen.

Sadness can leave us with a sense of despair and hopelessness; we may struggle to see that life has purpose. But God is able to heal this array of emotions. Your life *does* have purpose, and God's hope will sustain you and give you peace. Your emotions of sadness will heal, and in each struggle with hopelessness, God will rescue you and continuously journey with you (Isa. 43:2).

As you journey in your grief, my prayer is that you know God's mighty comfort and love for you (Heb. 13:5b). Also, my prayer is that you have the sweet assurance of knowing Jesus Christ as your wonderful Lord and Savior and one day seeing Him face to face in eternity.

Dear Heavenly Father,

Thank You for sheltering us in our journey of grief. Thank You, Lord, for healing our sadness as Your love embraces us in our tears. Thank You, Lord; we never journey alone in our grief. In the midst of our sadness, You are our constant companion, reminding us that we are never alone. I love You, Daddy!

Chapter 8

LONELINESS

Lord, Hold Me Until the Storm Passes Over

And the Lord, he it is that doth go before thee; he will be with thee, he will not fail thee, neither forsake thee: fear not, neither be dismayed.
—Deuteronomy 31:8

Oh, how at times I miss and long to embrace my most precious gentle giant, my son. I miss his beautiful smile and big, burly hug. It seems like yesterday that my precious son and I were sitting at the kitchen table laughing about the day's events or working together in ministry or hanging out. It seems like yesterday that I heard those words, "Mom, I love you." It seems like yesterday that Victor's arms tightly hugged me as he said, "Mom, I love you." It seems like yesterday that I heard him say, "Mom, do you need help?" or "Mom, let me share with you what the Lord is showing me." It seems like yesterday that I heard, "Mom, I have a problem. Pray for me," or held him and prayed for him earnestly, seeking God on behalf of my beloved son. Yet, there is a day coming when I will feel his loving embrace and hear his words, "I love you."

In sorrow, there is a loneliness that is difficult to define. It is a deep longing to have the void left by your loved one filled. I know the void my son left will not be filled until the Lord calls me home and I take my eternal journey. As we allow the Lord to journey with us, He will not allow this emptiness to destroy or consume us. His power and might give us hope in the midst of the pain of loneliness, enabling us not to be defeated by hopelessness.

God held me close and healed me, giving me purpose and strength for the journey (Jer. 29:11). Today God continues to journey with me, for He truly is my healer and my hope. He is my life (Col. 3:4).

There is coming a day…but until that time, I press on serving our Heavenly Father with all of my heart, strength, and breath, seeking to reach a hurting, lost, and dying world as our Heavenly Father gives me grace.

Abba Father; Daddy, thank You for my son Victor. Thank You, Lord, that You are his Messiah and he reigns with You today. Thank You that this life will pass and I will see my gentle giant again for all eternity, never to depart.

Lord, one day I will see Your face; I pray that I will hear you say, "Well done, My good and faithful servant." I love you, Victor. I love You, Daddy: My Heavenly Father. Thank You for Your faithfulness in saving Victor and giving him eternal life! (John 3:16)

Let's read Lamentations:

> This I recall to my mind, therefore have I hope. It is of the Lord's mercies that we are not consumed, because his compassions fail not. They are new every morning: great is thy faithfulness. The Lord is my portion, saith my soul; therefore will I hope in him.
>
> —Lamentations 3:21–24

God's mercies are new every morning:

- God loves you.
- God will take care of you.
- God will give you strength.
- God will show you loving mercy.

You will not be consumed:

- God will not forsake you.
- As you trust the Lord, the journey of grief will not consume or destroy you.
- Again, the journey of grief will not consume you.

Great is God's faithfulness:

- In life's storms
- In the heartaches of life
- In the healing of your grief
- In the provision of your needs
- In every area of your life

He is Lord Almighty and Redeemer of the sins of every man, woman, boy, and girl. He rescues us in the pain of our grief, and He desires to redeem us in our sinful state.

Loneliness can cause a state of despair, a sense of rejection and abandonment. The emotion of despair, rejection, and abandonment causes many individuals to feel unloved. Loneliness also can create walls of defeating thoughts, fear, despair, and anger.

► Does God forsake us in our loneliness or trials of life?

_____

_____

► Are you consumed in loneliness since the passing of a loved one?

_____

_____

► Has loneliness brought you into a state of hopelessness?

_____

_____

► Are you troubled by overwhelming emotions of loneliness, fear, and doubt? Please describe:

_____

_____

_____

> When you pass through the waters, I *will be* with you; and through the rivers, they shall not overflow you. When you walk through the fire, you shall not be burned, nor shall the flame scorch you.
> —Isaiah 43:2, nkjv

Often in sorrow many struggle with overwhelming emotions that can feel like crashing tidal waves. But as we trust the Lord, He is surely our anchor in the storm and will carry us through. During grief, the struggle of loneliness may be overwhelming which may cause us to isolate ourselves in the emotion of hopelessness. Sadly, in the despair of hopelessness, some may struggle to believe that God cares.

You are not alone (Lam. 3:21–24), though the reality of your struggle may seem to be overwhelming. God will surely heal your pain and you will smile again (Ps. 30:5b). How, you may ask? God is able to heal you in the depths of every struggle, fear, doubt, and wound that you may be struggling with and enable you to again have hope and purpose! (Jer. 29:11)

Often, those who are struggling with loneliness isolate themselves with defeating thoughts of:

- God does not love me.
- No one loves me.
- I am forsaken and abandoned.
- Everyone hates me.
- No one cares.
- I am a burden to others.
- I am worthless.
- I will die alone.
- I offend people.
- I am not worthy of being loved by God and others.

These defeating thoughts may cause:

- Depression
- Anger
- Despairing emotions
- Hopelessness
- Fear
- Defeat
- Unforgiveness
- Blame
- Emotions of feeling unloved
- Bitterness

- Despair
- Distrust
- Isolation

Please write scriptures concerning what the Lord states about these emotions:

▶ Depression:

▶ Anger:

▶ Despairing emotions:

▶ Hopelessness:

▶ Fear:

▶ Defeat:

▶ Unforgiveness and blame:

▶ Emotions of feeling unloved:

▶ Bitterness:

▶ Despair:

▶ Distrust:

▶ Isolation:

▶ Loneliness:

(**Excerpt:** *My Journey Home: Study Guide*)

QUESTIONS

1. Have you experienced the pain and struggle of loneliness?

2. Please describe how loneliness affects your life.

3. When you are afraid or have emotions of overwhelming loneliness, are you allowing God to intervene—or are you letting defeat have control of your heart? Please explain:

4. Do you feel that your loneliness is greater than God's intervention in comforting you? Please explain:

_____

_____

_____

5. Is there any situation in your life that you believe is greater than God (Luke 1:37)? Please explain:

_____

_____

_____

(Excerpt: *My Journey Home: Workbook*)

Often in our journey of life, sorrow, fears, and trials seem to creep in without notice, leaving us overwhelmed. As we become overwhelmed with loneliness, we struggle because the circumstances of life seem like giants. These struggles can cause us to lose our hope and peace. Yet, we run to our place of solitude, hoping to hide or find refuge from overwhelming emotions. Often we may flee to unstable places of refuge. The array of emotions can be like living in the tidal wave of a storm, feeling that the waves of the waters and storms will destroy us. Let's look at Matthew 8:23-27:

> Then he got into the boat and his disciples followed him. Suddenly, a furious storm came up on the lake, so that the waves swept over the boat. But Jesus was sleeping. The disciples went and woke him, saying, "Lord, save us! We're going to drown!" He replied, "You of little faith, why are you so afraid?" Then he got up and rebuked the winds and the waves, and it was completely calm. The men were amazed and asked, "What kind of man is this? Even the winds and the waves obey him!"
> —Matthew 8:23–27, niv

Suddenly and without warning, a furious storm began to affect the lives of the disciples. In fear they began to cry, "Lord, save us! We are going to drown!" Are we not sometimes like the disciples when we see the storms of life raging? Yet, as with the disciples, the Lord can calm the storms of our emotions.

> Then he got into the boat and his disciples followed him. Suddenly a furious storm came up on the lake, so that the waves swept over the boat. But Jesus was sleeping. The disciples went and woke him, saying, "Lord, save us! We're going to drown!" He replied, "You of little faith, why are you so afraid?" Then he got up and rebuked the winds and the waves, and it was completely calm. The men were amazed and asked, "What kind of man is this? Even the winds and the waves obey him!"
> —Matthew 8:23–27, niv

As God's children, we can rejoice because no matter what depths of loneliness exist in our lives, we are never alone or hopeless. God is faithful and compassionate. Our present sorrow and loneliness do not define our purpose, our hope, or our tomorrows. Life's difficult circumstances prepare us for God's great plan and purpose. God is a place of refuge and peace for His children because He is our true refuge. Emotions of loneliness may cause disbelief in God's promises, but God will calm the storms of our emotions and give us hope.

> Dear Heavenly Father,
> Thank You for Your faithfulness and love. Though at times our hearts yearn to see our loved one and loneliness comes; we are never alone.
> Thank You precious Heavenly Father, for You are forever our loving constant companion and friend. You are our song in the in the night (Ps. 42:8).

Have you ever felt hopeless as though the unbearable emotions of the passing of your loved one will win and your loneliness will become your sanctuary? Loneliness and hopelessness may leave us depleted and living in an array of emotions of despair. Yet the Lord's promises are true; and in your pain of loneliness and hopelessness, He is God and will never leave you nor forsake you. God sees your tears. You are never alone, and He is supreme Lord in your circumstances.

Remember, God will forever love you and will never leave nor forsake you; you will never journey alone. (Heb. 13:5).

QUESTIONS

- Does God provide us with rest and peace in our pain and loneliness as we look to Him and trust Him? Please explain:

- How do you see God's love as He journeys with you in your loneliness? Please explain:

- In the midst of your loneliness and pain do you believe that God has a plan for your life? (Jer. 29:11–14) Please explain:

- Many describe their loneliness like living in a cave, a dark place of great isolation and hopelessness. Do your emotions sometimes feel as though you are living in a cave of loneliness, hopelessness, and despair? Please explain:

- Have you ever felt that no one cared about your grief? Please explain:

- How did the Lord intervene and help you to embrace the truth that you are never alone? (Heb. 13:5)

_____

_____

_____

- How does the Lord comfort you in your loneliness?

_____

_____

_____

- How did or how is the Lord restoring your hope?

_____

_____

_____

- Do you believe that the Lord is able to restore your hope? Please explain:

_____

_____

_____

You Are Not Alone

In the journey of healing, you are most certainly not alone (Heb. 13:5b). God never leaves His children to journey alone. Though you may be struggling with emotions as confusing as a scattered puzzle, God will heal your wounded emotions and restore your joy. God will not fail you!

God is faithful, and He is able to comfort and deliver us in our loneliness. In our loneliness, we can cry out to the Lord, and He will meet us in our pain. The Lord is able to reach us in the depths of our caves or behind our wall of silence.

Our Heavenly Father greatly loves us and is not silent in our pain; He is our comforter. God will comfort us through His Spirit (2 Cor.1:1–7). We serve an awesome, supreme God, and He will not leave us nor forsake us (Heb. 13:5).

> It is of the Lord's mercies that we are not consumed, because his compassions fail not. They are new every morning: great is thy faithfulness. The Lord is my portion, saith my soul; therefore, will I hope in him.
> —Lamentations 3:22–24

We must not run from our pain and loneliness, but allow God to heal us. Though you may run from the loneliness that seems very difficult, God sees you and knows where you are. God's love will heal the wounded areas of your heart. Trust the Lord; He is able and does care about the loneliness and hopelessness that His children may encounter in their journey of grief.

As we seek the Lord and continuously place our fears, loneliness, hopelessness, and depression before Him, the Lord will set us free from the emotions that seemingly bind us.

Please:

1. Seek God.
2. Pray and acknowledge your loneliness, fears, pain, and hopelessness before the Lord.
3. Ask others to pray.
4. Be willing to pray, confess, and release these wounded emotions before the Lord and ask Him to reveal and heal all the areas of emotional pain that you are struggling with.
5. Ask God daily to enable you to heal emotionally (Isa. 41:13).
6. Ask God to enable you to move forward in His plans and purpose for you, one day at a time (Jer. 29:11–13).

As the Lord enables you to move forward by His grace, continue to trust Him as you encounter battles and trials (Luke 1:37). God, who is faithful, will enable you to prevail and move forth in the purpose He has for your life even when you have tears in your eyes! God can use our grief to strengthen us and build greater, productive pathways in our life! And God can use our pain to be a greater blessing to others.

The Lord will give you strength, grace, and endurance, and He will enable you to move forward. Though your heart has encountered sorrow, God is faithful and mighty. He can deliver you and give you hope and healing. The Lord will reach you in the depths of your sorrow and gently hold you through the storms in your life that you may encounter. You are never alone, and God who is your closest companion is able to turn your tears into joy (Ps. 30:5).

If you are in a journey of sorrow, know that one day your sorrow will pass and you will smile again. But, until that time, you are not journeying alone. Blessings!

> Dear Lord,
> I love You! Thank You, my precious Heavenly Father, for being my shelter where I will find comfort and hope. Thank You, Lord, that I am never alone, for You will never leave Your children to journey alone. For You are our anchor of peace and stronghold of love.

Chapter 9

SECLUSION

Lord, You Are My Hiding Place

Hear my cry, O God; attend unto my prayer. From the end of the earth will I cry unto thee, when my heart is overwhelmed: lead me to the rock that is higher than I.

—Psalm 61:1–2

The words echoed in my heart, "Victor has passed." My heart ached to believe that these words were not true. But with every waking day, the certainty of Victor's eternal journey became my reality.

But God! He is truly faithful and awesome. When words could not express the depths of my emotion and pain, He sustained and surrounded me in His love when it seemed the tidal waves of grief would prevail over me. When the question screamed from my heart, "How can I go on without my gentle giant?" God rescued me from the spiral of grief and pain—and held me.

The love and peace that I felt strengthened me greatly for the journey ahead. And throughout the journey, I felt God's embracing strength and peace as He carried me. He has enabled me to move forward in His love and strength; I truly have hope. Though I miss my precious Victor, I rejoice that I will see my son again. Until that blessed time, the Lord continues to embrace me with His peace, mercy, love, and strength.

During the earlier days of my journey of grief, it was like I had been set apart by the Lord in a place of indescribable peace where the Lord comforted and met with me. There I never felt alone. Though I wept, the Lord reminded me that I never weep alone. My son's passing was a time of grief, but I had a sweet assurance and joy knowing that I would see him again. Victor's home-going sparked in me a greater desire to tell a hurting, lost, and dying world that Jesus Christ saves and eternity waits for every believer.

We all grieve differently, and our emotions may differ as we find our place of refuge with the Father. As I sought God as my refuge through prayer and His Word, I truly found great comfort. In the midst of the saddest day of my life, God sustained me with His peace as He lovingly shelters me with love and strength in my journey of grief.

I found that I greatly needed times of isolation when I could draw away from the busyness of life and find my refuge in the Lord. The world was so busy around me, and I would cry out in my heart, "Lord, do they not know that my son has just passed?" Though I had wonderful family and friends, yet in the depths of my grief, only God could reach me. He continually assured me that I was not alone.

The Lord not only continually healed me, He sent those who would love and embrace me with His love. What a great and awesome God! God lovingly sends family and friends to minister to us, which is a tremendous blessing. Yes, as we find comfort in our Heavenly Father; relatives and friends may struggle to understand why we need to seclude ourselves with our Heavenly Father. Even greater, His peace and strength are crucial; they sustain us on this journey.

If you are isolated in a valley of despair, depression, and hopelessness, God truly wants to meet you there and heal your wounded heart. I affirm with my whole heart that you can trust the Lord; He will meet you in the very depths of your grief.

> Dear Lord,
> Thank You that I can bring my heart's sorrows to You as my strong tower and the place where I find love. Thank You, Lord. When my heart aches, You are my hiding place that shelters me in the journey of my healing. Thank You, Lord; in You I find shelter and love. You are the healer of my grieving, wounded heart. Lord, I rest in You (Heb. 13:5; Ps. 61:2).

You may ask, "How can God sustain me in the depths of my grief?"

- He is God and He is able to sustain you (Eph. 3:20).
- There is nothing impossible with God (Luke 1:37).
- God will comfort you (Zeph. 3:17).
- God will heal you (Ps. 30:2; 34).
- The Lord will be your song in the night (Ps. 42:8).
- The Lord will sing over you with songs of rejoicing (Zeph. 3:17).
- God loves you (Jer. 31:3).
- God will help (Ps. 28:7; Isa. 41:10).
- God will be your joy (Ps. 42:8).
- God is Lord, Savior, and Redeemer of the souls of every man, woman, boy, and girl (John 3:16).

Seclusion

God greatly loves you. Your sorrow will not overwhelm you (Isa. 43:2), but God will sustain and heal your broken heart. The Lord has said He will never leave nor forsake you (Heb.13:5), and forever His mercies are new every morning (Lam. 3:21–24). You are not alone, and you are not forsaken as you heal in your journey of grief. You are not alone.

QUESTIONS

▶ Do you isolate yourself from those you love as a form of shutting them out from your emotional pain? Please explain:

_____

_____

_____

▶ Are you struggling to have hope as you seek to live life day by day? Please explain:

_____

_____

_____

▶ Are you struggling to believe that someone truly cares about you and the emotions that you struggle with? (Isa. 49:15–16) Please describe:

_____

_____

_____

▶ Are you struggling to believe that God cares? (God does care about your grief and greatly loves you.) If yes, please explain:

_____

_____

_____

Do you live life in a prolonged and constant struggle to live each day, despairing at times of life itself? Please seek professional counseling if you feel this way. There are some in this journey who may need the intervention of counseling from a professional, biblically-based counselor.

Also, please discuss these struggles with family, friends, and your pastor. God is truly faithful, and in your journey of grief the Lord will never leave nor forsake you. He will continually journey with you; He never forsakes His children to journey alone in the pain, fears, and loneliness of grief.

▸ If you recently have had a loved one pass away, do you feel God's love as He embraces you in your journey? Please describe:

_____

_____

_____

▸ If your loved one's passing occurred many years ago, please describe your past and present journey with the Lord since that time.

_____

_____

_____

_____

As the Lord journeyed with me, He provided me with a beautiful host of loving family members and precious friends who loved and embraced me in the journey. As I ponder on these precious times I think about how the Lord gave my children Vincent and Tondra great strength as they took care of the various arrangements for Victor's "Celebration Day" and as Vincent preached on this precious day. I think about how my mother, who lives in another state, came quickly to be by my side; she too knows the pain of the passing of a son. I think of my sister, a lieutenant colonel, who held back her tears for fear that they would upset me; and I think of my precious friends, Maxine Holmes and Faye Frazier, who came daily to quietly pray for me.

My greatest times of strength and solitude, however, were with my Heavenly Father. These times gave me a haven of comfort and peace. The Lord surrounded me with the awesome presence of His peace. I love these restoring and refreshing times with the Lord. For some, finding a refuge in the Lord is difficult because of the struggle of pain, grief, and the array of emotions. If, in your journey of grief you are struggling to find the Lord as your refuge, please know that the Lord will meet you at the core of your grief and journey you through.

During this journey the Lord's greatness was revealed in my life, and His steadfast love, strength, and grace enabled me to journey on in His plans and purpose for my life (Jer. 29:11). The Lord truly was my anchor in the storms of the emotions of grief. As I rested in God's presence, there was hope as I sat and embraced this indescribable peace. Though at times I wept, the Lord comforted me as I rested and embraced His presence. These times of refuge with my Abba Father strengthened me.

Are you in a downward spiral of hopelessness and isolation, unable to move forward? Here are some simple steps that may be helpful in moving forward:

1. Pray
2. Seek and ask others to pray concerning any emotions that you are struggling with.
3. Seek and trust God to enable you to move from your walls of isolation.

As you seek the Lord; please:

- Acknowledge before the Lord your fears about moving out from the walls of isolation to the freedom of living a life of hope in Jesus Christ.
- Acknowledge before the Lord your reasons for isolating yourself from others.
- Acknowledge the security you find in being isolated from others.
- Acknowledge the unhealthy emotions that keep you within the walls of your isolation.
- Acknowledge any anger that you have toward:
  The Lord
  The loved one that passed
  Family
  Others
  Oneself

- Acknowledge any bitterness toward:
    - The Lord
    - The loved one that passed
    - Family
    - Others
    - Oneself

- Acknowledge any unforgiveness toward:
    - The loved one that passed
    - Family
    - Others
    - Oneself

- Acknowledge any wounded emotions of:
    - Shame
    - Defeating emotions
    - Loneliness
    - Depression
    - Despair
    - Sadness
    - Regret

- Acknowledge your insecurity within the walls of your hopelessness and sadness.

Please, continuously seek Jesus Christ to heal you in your grief and wounded emotions and enable you to move forward.

You Are Not Alone

Remember, moving forward is not forgetting the loved one who has passed, but pressing on in the purpose and plan that the Lord has for you (Phil 3:14)—and pressing on and being a vessel of God reaching a hurting, lost, and dying world. After Victor's passing, I was like a wounded child, and my Heavenly Father sheltered me from the storms and tidal waves of grief. Just as the Lord comforts us in our grief, one day His wonderful grace will enable us to comfort another who grieves. The grief that you may now be experiencing God will heal in time, for our God is *Jehovah Rapha*, our healer.

Though your faith may be the size of a mustard seed (Luke 17:6), as you trust God with all your heart, He will enable you to move from isolation to freedom. It may seem like you are only taking baby steps, but in childlike faith continually seek God, and He will enable you to move victoriously forward.

Also, please seek a pastor, biblical counselor, or trusted friend to walk with you during your journey from isolation to freedom. Prayerfully seek out others to pray for you daily, and trust God to send those who will faithfully journey with you. The Lord will surely heal your wounded emotions and journey with you through your grief and healing. The best will surely come. Though the storm may rage, through Jesus Christ you will find that there is truly sunlight after the storm.

Dear Lord,

I love You! Thank You for being my hiding place where I find strength and amazing love. Thank You Lord that I am never alone. In You alone I find strength and hope in the journey of life. Lord, may I faithfully serve and honor You as I continue to find in You amazing love and hope.

Chapter 10

DISBELIEF AND SHOCK

Lord, Is Victor Really Gone?

This I recall to my mind, therefore have I hope. It is of the LORD's mercies that we are not consumed, because his compassions fail not. They are new every morning: great is thy faithfulness.

—Lamentations 3:21–23

God's Mercies

When your life is touched by grief; the initial shock may be overwhelming. A cry of overwhelming grief may come from the very depths of your heart. Sometimes this cry becomes a moan because the pain is inexpressible, indescribable. For some it is like a horrible dream or nightmare that they cannot wake from. And for some, the shock and guilt of the words "if only" resound in their hearts. Suddenly, the disbelief of the passing of a loved one becomes the reality you must accept. And now your fears and wounded emotions begin to give rise to a host of doubts and questions. But God! He will heal you through this journey of the pain and shock of the passing of your loved one. God still has a plan and purpose for your life.

God's mercies are new every morning; breathe and know that in our weaknesses God makes us strong (2 Cor. 12:9); He is your anchor of strength and will enable you to move on—one moment, one day at a time.

Victor' passing was a great shock; often I would find myself saying, "My baby has truly passed from this life to life eternal." How quickly life passes! But when it is a child, spouse, family member, or close loved one who has passed, the feelings of disbelief and shock are amplified. These emotions can overwhelm you. Truly, the hope, strength, love, and grace of Jesus Christ strengthens us and enables us to stand. He is our anchor and our firm foundation. Praise God!

Though our hearts long to embrace our family member again, God's grace and love will defeat the almost overwhelming pain of the passing of our loved one. I know what it is like to have your heart long to awaken from this bad dream, from the pain of the loss of our treasured and precious loved one, from the regret or longing to have a second chance to do things differently. God does have an appointed day of eternity for every life. But Jesus Christ journeys with us; He carries us and heals the pain of our grieving heart.

We may ask, "Why, Lord?" But the Bible says that there is an appointed time of death for us all (Heb. 9:27). We must remember and embrace the fact that God makes no mistakes regarding the passing of our loved one. There is an appointed time for every life to journey from this life to eternity. As Christians we must reach those who remain in this life with the good news of salvation. Our prayer is that their home will be in eternity with Jesus Christ.

In the journey of grief, we grieve not like those who have "no hope" (1 Thess. 4:13). The appointed date of Victor's home-going came quickly and without notice. But God did not allow me to grieve as one with no hope, but as one with great *hope*. The Lord held me closely and ministered to my heart and the core of my emotions, giving me strength and great peace. Though we are separated by this life for a moment of time, I will surely see my gentle giant again (1 Thess. 4:13). The Bible says to be absent in the body is to be present with the Lord.

> We are confident, I say, and willing rather to be absent from the body, and to be present with the Lord.
> —2 Corinthians 5:8

As we move forward in our journey of healing, God will heal our many tears (Ps. 30:5b) and the deep longing for our loved ones who have passed from this life to life eternal. Often in the initial shock of the passing of a loved one, there are questions such as:

- Why?
- Is this a horrible dream?
- Is he / she really gone?

The shock of my son's home-going was one that I did not initially understand, but the Lord in His faithfulness lovingly journeyed with me—and for that I say, "Praise the Lord!" Many have found that keeping a journal of their journey of healing has been a tremendous blessing of hope and healing as they seek to help others in their journey.

Oh Lord! My heart cried out, "Is it true that my precious loved one has passed from this life to eternity?" Father, You make no mistakes. I embrace this truth amidst the questions of my heart.

Father, I trust You, knowing that You are my shelter as You journey with me in the healing of my grief. Thank You, Lord; I am never alone as Your love, peace, and mercy embrace me.

In your journey of healing, God never wastes the pain and the sorrow you encounter. God is faithful and can use your journey to comfort or encourage another.

> Blessed be the God and Father of our Lord Jesus Christ, the Father of mercies and God of all comfort, who comforts us in all our affliction so that we will be able to comfort those who are in any affliction with the comfort with which we ourselves are comforted by God.
> —2 Corinthians 1:3–4, nasb

In the following pages, please write about your journey. In the months or years to come, you will see healing and God's continued faithfulness in your life

- ▶ If you are comfortable and ready, please write your experience of the initial shock of the passing of your loved one.

_____

_____

_____

_____

_____

- ▶ Please write how God has used your journey to strengthen you in your relationship with Him.

_____

_____

_____

- ▶ Has God used your journey to change your life in any area?

_____

▸ Did your journey strengthen your dependency on the Lord?

▸ Did God use your journey to help others in their grief?

Often we forget that our journey of grief can enable us to reach others with the same compassion and love that the Lord Himself has shown us. Since Victor's passing, the Lord has opened many doors that have enabled me to reach those who feel forsaken in their storm of grief. The Lord has enabled me to reach those in prison, the homeless, the broken, and the unsaved with healing and the hope of eternity through Jesus Christ. He has helped me reach the grieving hearts of those who have lost hope and need someone who will lovingly walk with them. I assure them that they are loved, that Jesus Christ cares and sees their tears, and that He is able to heal their sorrow (Ps. 30:5b).

Are you willing to minister to those who are grieving with the comfort that you have found in Jesus Christ?

> Blessed *be* the God and Father of our Lord Jesus Christ, the Father of mercies and God of all comfort, who comforts us in all our affliction so that we will be able to comfort those who are in any affliction with the comfort with which we ourselves are comforted by God.
> —2 Corinthians 1:3–4, nasb

Perhaps in time you will reach a hurting, lost, and dying world with the same hope and comfort in Jesus Christ that you have embraced. If you cannot go out to them, please pray for those who are in a journey of grief and pain.

Our journey of life is never wasted; the Lord will use every tear and sorrow. You can be a blessing, strength, and hope in the life of someone else who is traveling a similar road. Your journey can be the greatest blessing for others who are struggling.

Has your journey given you more…

- Compassion?

_____

_____

_____

- Empathy? (Empathy enables you to relate to another individual's pain due to your also having the same journey in life.)

_____

_____

_____

- Sympathy? (Sympathy enables you to have compassion for another individual's pain though you have not had the same journey in life.)

_____

_____

_____

- Patience?

_____

_____

- Love?

_____

_____

- Has your journey strengthened your faith?

- Has your journey given you more love for our Heavenly Father?

- Please describe God's faithfulness to you in this journey:

> So do not fear, for I am with you; do not be dismayed, for I am your God. I will strengthen you and help you; I will uphold you with my righteous right hand.
> —Isaiah 41:10, NIV

Whether your journey is currently full of weeping and tears or is beginning to see the fullness of God's healing, please be encouraged. Whatever your stage of grief, God will not forsake you; He will heal your broken, grieving, and lonely heart. God greatly loves you, dear one (Zeph. 3:17).

> *Dear Lord,*
>
> *Thank You! For You are my healer, sustainer, and strength. Thank You for Your great love as You hold me in the midst of the storm. Thank You, my healer, for I will yet soar as the eagles as I find my refuge in You and You alone.*

Chapter 11

ANGER

Lord, Heal Me in My Anger

My dear brothers and sisters, take note of this: Everyone should be quick to listen, slow to speak and slow to become angry, because human anger does not produce the righteousness that God desires.

—James 1:19–20, niv

Sadly, many struggle with anger over the passing of a loved one. Some struggle with anger toward God, without acknowledging that for every life born into this world there is an appointed time of passing. Yet, this appointed time is eternal, whether one has chosen to be with our Heavenly Father or to be eternally separated: hell.

Since Victor's home-going, I have often been asked if I became angry at any point. And I must state that during my journey of grief, by the grace of God, I did not have emotions of anger. God used the following scriptures to greatly comfort me: 2 Corinthians 5:8; 1 Thessalonians 4:13; and Hebrews 9:27. As God comforted my heart with His Word, my heart was at peace. Many asked me if I was angry at God because my son was taken away so young, but my reply was that it was God's appointed time for Victor's passing to his eternal home, and that I will surely see him again (Heb. 9:27). Hallelujah! Praise God!

> *Dear Lord,*
> *Please strengthen me in my pain. Heavenly Father, may my heart be covered by Your love. Please enable me to seek Your face in my anger and array of emotions. Lord, please continuously heal me and set my heart free from the pain of sorrow.*

Many struggle with the emotions of anger during their journey of grief, but *prolonged anger* can become a vicious cycle of destructive emotions if intervention does not take place or if the individual does not process this anger and move forward.

When you struggle with prolonged anger during your journey of grief, this anger can lead to bitterness, rage, depression, resentment, and hopelessness. These destructive emotions can cause you to isolate yourself behind a wall that both victimizes and defeats you. Remember, depression is often characterized by overwhelming emotions of despair, hopelessness, and defeat. Also, with continuous despairing emotions of depression, one may have thoughts of suicide. At times, there are those in this journey who may need the intervention of counseling from a professional biblically-based counselor.

I have listened to the stories of many individuals whose children have passed from this life to eternity; they live in great grief, often reliving with me the day of their child's passing. In some cases the child passed away many years ago. Nevertheless, the love of a parent is deep, and the passing of a child can leave a void that never heals. Some of these parents live daily in hopelessness and despair.

God's love, grace, mercy; and strength are deeper than the deepest pain or heartaches. God is truly able to heal the broken and grieving heart.

QUESTIONS

- ▶ Are you struggling with anger over the passing of a loved one? Please explain:

_____

_____

_____

- ▶ Are you struggling with *prolonged anger* over the passing of a loved one? Please explain:

_____

_____

_____

- ▶ Do you believe that the passing of your loved one was too soon? (Heb. 9:27) Please explain:

_____

_____

_____

Anger

▶ Are you wondering if God made a mistake, or if it was God's appointed time?

Yes

_____

No

_____

▶ Please explain:

_____

_____

_____

> The Lord is gracious and compassionate, slow to *anger* and rich in love.
> —Psalm 145:8, NIV

If you find that you live life in a state of prolonged and constant anger, please seek counseling from a professional, biblically-based counselor. Also, please discuss these struggles with family, friends, and your pastor. God is truly faithful, and in your journey of grief, the Lord will never leave nor forsake you. The Lord will continually journey with you in the anger, pain, fears, and loneliness of your grief.

▶ Please describe your anger:

_____

_____

_____

▶ Have you allowed your anger to cause you to despair and lose hope? Please describe:

_____

_____

_____

- Have you allowed your anger to cause you to become bitter? Please describe:

  _____
  _____
  _____

- Have you allowed your anger to cause you to become enraged? Please describe:

  _____
  _____
  _____

- Have you allowed your anger to cause you to become depressed? Please describe:

  _____
  _____
  _____

- How has your anger affected your relationship with God?

  _____
  _____
  _____

- How has your anger affected your relationship with your family?

  _____
  _____
  _____

- How has your anger affected your relationship with your friends?

  _____

- How has your anger affected your ability to be salt and light in the lives of those who are in your life? Please explain:

- Do you feel like one living behind walls of pain, taken captive by anger? Please explain:

- Do you feel like you are struggling behind a wall of wounded and destructive emotions? Please explain:

- How has your anger hindered your emotional healing in your journey of healing? Please explain:

Please allow the Lord to help you release your anger so that your life can again have meaning. Your prolonged anger is a hindrance to God's plan and purpose for your life. Your life does have great meaning! As you allow the Lord to journey with you in your journey of grief, you will surely see that your life has meaning and purpose.

Are you willing to release your anger and have hope? Though many seek to be released from the constant downward spiral of anger, they live constantly in the bondage of anger. But God is able to release and set you free from the downward spiral of anger. Please, prayerfully surrender your anger to the Lord.

Releasing Prolonged Anger

Let's review a few steps that will be helpful in releasing prolonged anger. The greatest source of healing is Jesus Christ; He has great power to heal. His gift of salvation and forgiveness for sin is even greater, providing hope and eternal life.

1. Please pray, trusting the Lord to heal you.
2. Seek a friend or counselor who will journey with you in your healing.
3. *Acknowledge your prolonged anger or rage* (1 John 1:9).
4. Admit your anger and the behavior and emotion that you struggle with because of your anger.
5. *Acknowledge the cause of your anger* (Eph. 4:31).
6. Admit to the Lord the cause of your anger (if you cannot define the cause of your anger, ask the Lord to reveal it to you).
7. *Acknowledge why you are angry* (Heb. 4:16).
8. Seek the Lord with all of your heart (Prov. 3:5).
9. Pour out your heart before the Lord concerning your anger and your pain, disappointment, fears; and despair (Heb. 4:16).
10. Repent of all sin and negative behavior that your anger may have caused (1 John 1:9).
11. *Surrender to the Lord* (Gal. 2:20)
12. Surrender your life to Jesus Christ new and afresh.

Dear Lord,

In You I find hope, forgiveness, and deliverance. Father, please continually set me free from the emotions of anger. May I continually embrace the fact that

You are my peace. You, Lord, are the rescuer of wounded emotions and will never stop loving me (John 10:10; 14:27).

Again, if you are not saved, repent and be saved. The greatest source of healing is Jesus Christ and His power to heal. But even greater is the gift of salvation and forgiveness of sins, giving hope and eternal life.

(Excerpt: My Journey Home: Jesus Christ the Rescuer of Wounded Emotions)

- First: God loves you (Rom. 5:8–9).
- Second: All have sinned (Rom. 3:10–12, 23).
- Third: Sin separates us from God (Rom. 6:23).
- Fourth: God desires to be your Heavenly Father and spend eternity with you (Rev. 3:20; John 1:12; 3:16).

You may ask how you can have this relationship with God through Jesus Christ our Lord:

1. Repent of your sin (Acts 3:19).
2. Believe that Jesus Christ died and rose again that you can have eternal life (John 3:16; 15:13).
3. Repent and receive Jesus Christ as your Lord and Savior. Ask Him to come into your heart as Savior (John 1:12; Rom. 3:20).
4. Allow Jesus Christ to rule over your life (Gal. 2:20); He will do amazing things in your life.

Lord Jesus Christ, please forgive me of my sins, save my soul, and give me eternal life. I believe that You died on the cross for my sins and were resurrected again that I may have eternal life. I repent of all my sins. Please Lord Jesus Christ, come into my heart and become Lord of my life. Take total control of my life; I surrender (Gal. 2:20) my life to You. Thank You, Lord Jesus Christ, for Your love in receiving my prayer and saving my soul. In Jesus' name, I pray. Amen.

Are You Willing?

Anger is a downward spiral of destruction causing you and those around you pain. If anger is your constant companion, it can isolate you and cause stagnation. You must be willing to release this anger in order to truly heal.

God is able to move you from your ensnarement of bondage of prolonged anger. Though you may struggle in your prolonged anger, hidden behind the walls of regret and destructive emotions, God can set you free. How, you may ask? Trust God, for He is able to minister, heal, and journey with you in your journey of grief. God is able to minister to the broken and barren areas of your heart and give you hope. God will enable you to forgive—whether it is yourself or others. God is able to set you *free!*

You may state that you have embraced the emotion of anger for many years and are not able to release your anger. But God! Again, He can and will heal your anger and set you free from the pain and destructive bondage of prolonged anger.

The Lord will heal you in the depths of your grief and pain as you seek the Lord. He can surely heal you and journey with you in your grief. The Lord will also heal you in the barren and wounded areas of your heart (Heb. 13:5).

> *Dear Lord,*
>
> *Please heal my anger and enable me to forgive others or myself. Lord, enable me to see that Your will is perfect in a hurting, lost, and dying world. Father, You make no mistakes. Enable me to embrace Your Word and Your truth, and nothing I could have done would have changed my loved one's passing during their appointed time. Lord, may my heart resound with Your faithfulness and goodness. Thank You for greatly loving me. Praise the Lord!*

Chapter 12

WORRY

Lord, I Am Afraid and Worried. How Does Life Continue?

*I will both lay me down in peace, and sleep: for
thou, LORD, only makest me dwell in safety.*
—Psalm 4:8

Shortly after Victor's home-going, my heart began to ponder the void his home-going had left in my life. Yet, I struggled with Victor no longer being a beautiful presence within our home; I truly missed the presence of my gentle giant, his words of encouragement and godly wisdom, and his warm hugs. I missed giving him a mother's kisses. Victor was my joy, and we would laugh for hours at the day's events.

I was often asked if I was going to sell the home where Victor had lived with me; others questioned whether I should live alone. They did not understand that I was never alone; I had nothing to fear because the Lord keeps me in His constant care (Isa. 49:15–16).

Until adulthood, I would hold Victor close to my heart as I kissed and held him tightly…until the day of his passing on to his heavenly home. God greatly sustained me on the day of Victor's home-going and continues to sustain me. Fear was not my constant companion, but I struggled over the void my precious child had left and my life changing so quickly due to the reality of his home-going. I no longer saw his physical presence or experienced his love. However, I did gain a greater faith by steadfastly knowing that Victor's Savior is Jesus Christ and that he surely, with great joy, lives with Him today. God's awesome love and care surrounded me whenever I struggled with the emptiness of Victor's passing. God continuously reminded me that I was not alone; He let me know that He greatly loved me and would forever journey with me.

When I cried out to the Lord in prayer and faith, I rested in the loving care of my Heavenly Father and joy of His sweet assurance that I would see my gentle giant again. There will be a day when my life will be with Victor and other loved ones in Heaven for eternity. *Even more precious, I will see my Jesus face to face for eternity.*

Dear Lord,

Thank You that I can run in Your presence with my arms full of the worries of this world and give them to You as You bear my burdens and remind me that "all is well."

Thank You, Lord, that in those moments You always faithfully remind me that You have been with me all the time protecting, providing for, and sheltering me.

Thank You, Lord, that Your children are never alone…no, never alone.

With Victor's passing, I miss the blessing of *his* precious

- Smile
- Loving ways
- The joy of hearing him say, "Mom, I love you."
- Daily laughter
- Encouraging words
- Words encouraging me to "press on" in ministry for Jesus Christ
- Always seeking to put the Lord first and my needs
- Selfless ways
- Unconditional love
- "Mom, are you OK?"
- "Mom, let's hang out."
- "Mom, plan a vacation and let's go."
- "Mom, can I help you?"
- "Mom, do you need me for anything?"
- "Mom, pray about that decision before you move forward."
- "Mom, let God fight your battles."

Victor loved me with a selfless love, seeking to be the hands and feet of Jesus Christ and seeking to love and serve others. But though I miss my gentle giant and his beautiful presence, the Lord reminds me that He is my:

- Savior and Redeemer
- Trusted Friend
- Life

- Living Water
- Hope in hopelessness
- Provider
- Comfort
- Joy
- Healer
- Deliverer
- Constant Companion
- Purpose
- Strength
- Laughter
- Faithful One
- Peace
- Counselor
- Healer
- Abba Father, Daddy
- Hiding Place
- Love of my life
- Husband
- Helper
- Forgiver of my sins
- Anchor in the storms of life
- Joy in sadness

When you have a void due to the passing of a loved one, often you cry out for sustaining hope and a refuge from the pain. The pain—and for some, despairing emotions—can cause many to live in the darkness of hopelessness.

But God!

Truly, He is able to reach the core of these emotions for those struggling in despair of darkness and give sustaining hope. We are never alone, and God is able to move us out of the pain of despair and darkness; He delivers us out of the miry clay (Ps. 40:1–3).

- ▶ Does your life have a void that cannot be filled since the home-going of your loved one? Please explain:

- ▶ If there is a heartfelt void since the passing of your loved one, how would you define this void? Please explain:

- ▶ Have you trusted Jesus Christ to fill this void? Please explain:

- ▶ What is your greatest struggle since the passing of your loved one? Please explain:

▶ How long have you been struggling with grief for your loved one? Please explain:

_____
_____
_____
_____
_____

▶ What emotions are you struggling with in your journey of grief? Please describe:

_____
_____
_____
_____

▶ Where do you find your greatest comfort in your journey of grief? Please explain:

_____
_____
_____
_____
_____

▶ Where do you find your greatest peace in your journey of grief? Please explain:

_____
_____

- Do you feel others understand your journey of grief? Please explain:

- Do you feel God understands your pain? Please explain:

But God! He knows our tomorrow and our pain, and His ways are perfect. Yet, greater, the Lord plans our way, and though we may not understand the path of grief, God does not forsake us as He journeys with us. We must always remember that God's ways are not our ways (Isa. 55:8–9). There is an appointed time of eternity for every life (John 3:16).

> But now, this is what the Lord says—he who created you, Jacob, he who formed you, Israel: "Do not fear, for I have redeemed you; I have summoned you by name; you are mine. When you pass through the waters, I will be with you; and when you pass through the rivers, they will not sweep over you. When you walk through the fire, you will not be burned; the flames will not set you ablaze. For I am the Lord your God.
> —Isaiah 43:1–3, NIV

In the journey of grief and in the storms of life, God has taught me that:

1. *He never leaves us alone* in the storms and turbulent times of life (Heb. 13:5). When we walk through the difficulties of life, God

journeys with us and sees us through to the other side of victory. *We are never alone!*

2. *Nothing takes God by surprise, no nothing* (Jer. 1:5). God knew us before we were born; He knows our days and the heartaches, battles, and trials that we may encounter. God is faithful, and He never fails His children in the battles of life. His plans and purposes for our lives are *perfect*; surely He is our awesome and mighty God!

3. *God heals our broken hearts* (Ps. 34), *sees our tears* (Ps. 30:5b), *and binds up our wounds* (Ps. 147:3). God will heal the wounds of His children and give them continued hope and strength to press on!

4. *We are never in despair in our trials*; for our God is mighty, and there is nothing impossible with Him (Luke 1:37). God will give us peace and comfort in our despair (John 14:27; 2 Cor. 1:5).

Yet, we must continue in God's mission of reaching lost souls that they would be saved! Even in the sorrows or heartaches of life, the great commission must continue as we seek to be salt and light to a hurting, lost, and dying world that is perishing into an eternal hell. We must reach the lost so they will have hope, know our Redeemer, Jesus Christ, and be saved.

The emptiness that follows the passing of a loved one may be great, but God is the great healer and will continually strengthen you and give you hope. Yes, our lives will change and in some aspects will never be the same, but by God's grace *we can press on and press forward* (Phil. 4:13). God will journey with us and again bring us victoriously to the other side. *Praise the Lord!* God Almighty knows our tomorrows, and His ways are perfect The Lord plans our way (Jer. 29:11), though we may not understand the path of grief or the home-going of our loved one. *God Almighty will journey with us until our very last breath; eternity awaits our glorious homecoming!*

> *Dear Precious Lord,*
>
> *Thank You, faithful God, that I can bring all my heart before You in prayer—my fears, insecurities, and the worries of my heart. Lord, though I do not know what tomorrow will bring, You are my faithful companion who will bring me through to the other side.*

Chapter 13

LONGING

Oh Lord, My Heart Yearns for My Loved One! Will My Life Ever Be the Same?

As I write this, I ponder the early days of my precious son's passing. My heart longed to hold him again and tell Victor these four words, "Son, I love you." How I have yearned to hear the front door open and my gentle giant say, "Mom, I am home." I miss sitting at the kitchen table for what seemed like hours, talking about his day, or laughing about the silliest things. I truly rejoice that Victor, my son and friend, will forever be in my heart, and I cherish those moments with him. But how I rejoice that separation from my son is temporary—for heaven awaits, and I will see Victor again. And with blessed assurance, I will see Jesus Christ my Savior face to face, never to depart! Hallelujah, what a day of rejoicing that will be! I know that my heart will always have those deep yearning moments, days, or seasons for my precious son Victor, but God forever sustains me and enables me to press on (Phil. 3:13–14).

God Is Faithful in Our Yearning

In the struggle to make sense of life; the deep yearning for a loved one may cause the journey to be increasingly difficult. But God is our deliverer and enables us to take one day at a time, to heal (Ps. 34), and to move forward. Please, rest and trust in the Lord and do not worry about your life, for He will not leave you to journey alone (Matt. 6:25–34).

Though our seasons of life may be may be difficult, *El Roi*, "The God who sees," will never leave or forsake us (Heb. 13:5). God sees our tears. As we trust the Lord, His love and strength will give us grace to press on in the midst of our deep yearning, love, and longing for our loved one. For our Lord God is able.

Until that time when I see my son again, will my life ever be the same? The answer is no. I must not dwell on the yesterdays of my life with my son, but on the blessed eternity with my son and in the Father's arms which are yet to come. Also, I must by the grace of God move forward to reach a hurting, lost, and dying world (Matt. 28:1–20) so that those who are unsaved may be saved. One day I will take my last breath and pass from this life into indescribable joy with my Heavenly Father forever and ever.

> *Dear Lord,*
>
> *Though my heart at times yearns for my precious loved one; yet, Lord, I embrace Your promises that You will never leave or forsake me. Though their appointed time has come, I thankfully embrace Your presence of comfort and love.*
>
> *Thank You, Lord, that You hold and shelter me until the storm passes over as I continuously rest in Your promises and the hope that I have in You.*

So do not fear, for I am with you; do not be dismayed, for I am your God. I will strengthen you and help you; I will uphold you with my righteous right hand.
—Isaiah 41:10, niv

Questions

▶ Do you wake up in the early morning hours troubled with thoughts that you cannot go on? Please explain:

_____

_____

_____

▶ God loves you and will never leave or forsake you (Heb. 13:5); He will forever journey with you until your last breath. Please respond:

_____

_____

_____

▶ Do you struggle to have purpose? (Jer. 29:11–13) Please explain:

_____

_____

_____

▶ Do you struggle to believe that God loves you? (Jer. 31:3) Please explain:

___

___

___

▶ Do you cry out, "Why am I still alive?" Please explain:

___

___

___

If one or more of these questions have troubled your heart or mind, know that you are not alone. Many individuals struggle to believe that life has purpose for them after the passing of a loved one, *but as long as you have breath, you have life. You have purpose!*

You are not alone in your journey of grief. As His child, God will never allow you to journey alone. You can be honest before the Lord with your emotions of grief, loneliness, and fear. God truly does hear the prayers of His children (Ps. 34:4–7).

> Therefore I tell you, do not worry about your life, what you will eat or drink; or about your body, what you will wear. Is not life more than food, and the body more than clothes? Look at the birds of the air; they do not sow or reap or store away in barns, and yet your heavenly Father feeds them. Are you not much more valuable than they? Can any one of you by worrying add a single hour to your life?
>
> And why do you worry about clothes? See how the flowers of the field grow. They do not labor or spin. Yet I tell you that not even Solomon in all his splendor was dressed like one of these. If that is how God clothes the grass of the field, which is here today and tomorrow is thrown into the fire, will he not much more clothe you—you of little faith? So do not worry, saying, 'What shall we eat?' or 'What shall we drink?' or 'What shall we wear?' For the pagans run after all these things, and your heavenly Father knows that you need them. But seek first his kingdom and his righteousness, and all these things will be given to you as well. Therefore do not worry about tomorrow, for tomorrow will worry about itself. Each day has enough trouble of its own.
>
> —Matthew 6:25–34, niv

Hebrew 13:5a: Remember, when we are fearful of our future: God will never leave or forsake us.

▶ What is your greatest fear about your future? Why?

_____

_____

Psalm 61:1–2: When as God's children, we struggle and are fearful of the future, God who is our Rock will sustain us.

▶ What is your greatest struggle about the future? Why?

_____

_____

Matthew 28:20: Again, God will not forsake His children; He will be with us until the end of time.

▶ Do you struggle with loneliness?

Yes

_____

No

_____

▶ Are there days that you are consumed with feelings of worthlessness and hopelessness?

Yes

_____

No

_____

Many struggle with the strength and hope to move forward after the passing of a loved one. God is faithful! He will strengthen you at the very point of your painful emotions of fear, anger, worthlessness, loneliness, hopelessness, and depression. For some, it may seem like the healing process is made up of many baby steps. For others, the healing process of grief moves forward much more rapidly. But if you are consumed with grief as one who lives life in despair and hopelessness, you will truly struggle to move forward. Some who are struggling to move forward may need the intervention of counseling from a professional biblically-based counselor.

My Gentle Giant

My son Victor lived with me and had never married, though he prayed for years for a wife. We planned fun activities together. We often prayed together and sought godly wisdom from one another. Victor was not only my oldest son, but my good friend.

After my son passed, I recognized the void his passing left in my heart and the sadness I felt as I revisited places that he and I had once frequented. God did not leave me in my sadness, but strengthened my heart and truly gave me hope.

> Do you not know? Have you not heard? The Lord is the everlasting God, the Creator of the ends of the earth. He will not grow tired or weary, and his understanding no one can fathom. He gives strength to the weary and increases the power of the weak. Even youths grow tired and weary, and young men stumble and fall...
> —Isaiah 40:28–31, NIV

Through my process of healing, the Lord renewed my strength, and I began to take baby steps toward revisiting the places where Victor and I had laughed, prayed, and listened to each other's journey of faith.

The question may linger in your heart, "Will my life ever be the same?" As Ecclesiastes 3:1–8 states, there are seasons in each of our lives that change. Yes, your life will differ or change. The void that the passing of your loved one brought may continue to remain, but Jesus Christ will be your faithful companion in your journey of grief. He will give you great strength and peace beyond measure. The Lord in time will increase your joy in the sorrow (Ps. 30:5), though at times it may seem that you live out daily the pain and grief of the passing of your loved one.

> The Lord thy God in the midst of thee is mighty; he will save, he will rejoice over thee with joy; he will rest in his love, he will joy over thee with singing.
> —Zephaniah 3:17

Be of good cheer; God will never leave or forsake you in your pain. He will strengthen you and give you hope. We never journey alone (Heb. 13:5). No, your life will never be the same, but God will heal your pain and carry you through this season of your journey. God will strengthen you to continue in the purpose for your life even in those times when you move forward with tears in your eyes. He will enable you to have joy (Zeph. 3:17).

Truly, God is faithful beyond measure! Today, as I reflect on God's awesome faithfulness and goodness, I can only say, "Thank You, Lord, for You are *Lord*, and You are good!" This year will be the fourth year since my gentle giant's home-going. To say that I have those moments when I miss my gentle giant is truly an understatement. But God! But God! He is faithful and sustains, encourages, embraces, and strengthens us with hope and peace beyond measure! By the grace of God, when scheduled to leave for India two months after Victor had gone home to be with the Lord, I awoke up expectantly at two o'clock in the morning and lifted the emotions of my heart to heaven. "Lord, I miss Victor," I told Him. The Lord clearly spoke to my heart and said, "Rita, do you want to be with Victor, or do you want to complete the journey?" I then lifted my hand and my heart to heaven and said, "Lord, I want to complete the journey." In the journey of life we encounter sorrow, trials, wounds from loved ones, and disappointments, but I encourage every believer not to quit, because the best is yet to come! Though we may have promises that are not yet fulfilled, though the journey of trials continues, though what you never expected is now your reality, God is greater, and God is able; and God is good! One day we will take our last breath, and suddenly those who have passed on in Christ we will see. And we will see the joyful harvest of all those years of serving the Lord when we sowed in tears and toils. Until that time, by God's loving mercy, let's complete the journey that He has for us. Through the Holy Spirit, let us armor ourselves with the Armor of God (Eph. 6:10–19) and a committed heart and go forth, for God will forever journey with us and use our lives greatly for His glory (Isa. 41:10; Luke 1:37).

Dear Lord,

I praise and thank You for being my comforter. Through the journey of life, you have faithfully been my strength, hope, and deliverer; You are my closest companion and the love of my life.

Thank You, Lord, for giving me hope, for You are my life and my faithful companion until I pass from this life to life eternal. Then I will embrace my faithful Father.

Chapter 14

REGRET

Lord, Heal Me of My Regrets

*For if our heart condemn us, God is greater than
our heart, and knoweth all things.*

—1 John 3:20

On October 11, 2010, my son Victor arrived home from work and fixed a quick meal. After he finished eating, he announced that he was leaving to go and pick up my grandson who needed a ride home from football practice; Victor had agreed to pick him up the previous day. I stated to him that he needed to rest since he had worked third shift as a program specialist, but Victor replied that he had given my grandson his word. What a joy and blessing that I taught my children the importance of integrity! Keeping one's word or promise is a matter of integrity; Victor lived this out until his last day here on Earth. As Victor prepared to leave, I put my arms around him and prayed. After I prayed for Victor, I kissed his bearded cheek and told him that I loved him. Victor then kissed my cheek and said, "Mom, I love you."

Suddenly, only a few hours later, my journey of grief and healing had begun. During my season of healing, I questioned if I should have driven my car to pick up my grandson instead of going to my scheduled appointment that day. The Lord enabled me to embrace the truth of His Word that God knew my precious son's days on earth (Ps. 37:18). His eternity was appointed for him on October 11, 2010 (Heb. 9:27). Yet, God in His mercy has strengthened me and given me hope.

But praise God, this separation is not final. Until I see my gentle giant again, by God's wonderful grace, I press on reaching a hurting, lost, and dying world with God's Word in my hands and in my heart. October 11, 2010, was God's appointed time for Victor's home-going to his eternal home. Praise God our momentary separation is not final! Hallelujah!

Again, the Bible says:

- Hebrews 9:27: There is an appointed time. Though my son's appointed eternity with the Father came suddenly for me, God's grace was greatly sufficient.
- 1 Thessalonians 4:13: We have hope. Though I grieved over the passing of my son; I did not grieve without hope.
- Hebrews 9:27: Hope after death. I find joy and comfort in knowing that my son had received Jesus Christ as His Lord and Savior and lives with Him today.

Oh Lord, I trust You with my struggles of regret. Lord, my heart cries out as I seek Your face, rescuer of my pain. Thank You, Heavenly Father, for embracing me in my pain and healing me. Thank You, Lord; You alone set the captive free and rescue us in our shame, regret, and pain. Thank You, Lord our healer.

QUESTIONS

This I recall to my mind, therefore have I hope. It is of the Lord's mercies that we are not consumed, because his compassions fail not. They are new every morning: great is thy faithfulness.
—LAMENTATIONS 3:21–23

▶ Are you struggling with regret? Please explain:

_____
_____
_____

▶ Are you regretting past negative actions that you took toward someone who has passed? If yes, please explain:

_____
_____
_____

- ▶ Have you allowed the Lord to help you to forgive yourself or release the self-condemnation that you may be embracing in your heart? Please explain:

_____

_____

_____

> For if ye forgive men their trespasses, your heavenly Father will also forgive you: but if ye forgive not men their trespasses, neither will your Father forgive your trespasses.
> —Matthew 6:14–15

- ▶ Are you struggling with unforgiveness or an unloving attitude toward a loved one who has passed? Please explain:

_____

_____

_____

- ▶ Do you blame someone else for the grief and regret that you are feeling? If so, why?

_____

_____

_____

- ▶ Have you sought the Lord to enable you to forgive them? Please explain:

_____

_____

_____

- ▶ Do you feel that if you had taken a particular action it might have intervened and prolonged their life? If yes, please explain:

_____

_____

_____

Though we may greatly love and miss our loved one, yearning to embrace them again and grieving their home-going, we cannot intervene or stop the appointed day (Heb. 9:27) of our loved one's passing. The Lord has an appointed day upon which every life will pass from this life into eternity. Remember, those who have received Jesus Christ as Lord and Savior will rejoice in heaven with our Heavenly Father as they embrace His presence and love for eternity. Yet, those who have rejected the gift of eternal life through Jesus Christ will sadly spend eternity separated from the Lord.

God is our comforter and our peace. Please review the following scriptures as they relate to God's faithfulness to be our comfort and peace.

- Lamentations 3:21–23; John 14:27
- Zephaniah 3:17; Psalm 4:8
- Psalm 29:11; Isaiah 26:3
- Isaiah 54:10; Jeremiah 29:11
- John 16:33; Romans 15:11–13
- 1 Corinthians 1:1–3; 2 Corinthians 1:2–5

At times during the journey of grief you may struggle with overwhelming emotions of regret. Also, during this journey of healing, you may need the intervention of counseling from a professional, biblically-based counselor.

PSALM 34
STEPS TO HEALING REGRET

1. *Seek* the Lord with your regretful heart and emotional pain.
2. *Cry out* to the Lord.
3. *Ask* the Lord to heal you; and surely the Lord will heal your broken heart.
4. *Repent* of the sin that has caused your wounded spirit and emotions of condemnation (1 John 1:9).
5. *Release* the pain of your past to the Lord.

6. *Trust* God to enable you to move forward.
7. *Embrace* a family member, pastor, or trusted friend to journey with you as the Lord lovingly enables you to continuously heal your journey of grief.

The Lord is faithful as He ministers to the pain and brokenheartedness of His children with His great love and His Word. God seeks for His children to trust Him in the seasons of brokenness. God is able; trust Him! He sets the captives free.

You cannot change what has happened, but you can seek God's forgiveness (1 John 1:9) and trust Him that your negative actions or other behaviors from your past will not again wound another individual as He enables you to be more like Jesus. God helps you by His love to forgive yourself, and through His Spirit, He enables you to freely love others.

> For if our heart condemn us, God is greater than our heart, and knoweth all things. Beloved, if our heart condemn us not, then have we confidence toward God.
> —1 John 3:20–21

When you are ensnared in the emotions of regret, painful and hopeless emotions often leave you defeated and broken. Many live in the ruins of regret and become stagnant, unable to move forward. We all can experience these seasons of regret. But God is our healer. Are you struggling with regret, sin, or an action from your past? Remember that God forgives and is able to deliver you from the bondage of regret. Remember that you are not alone.

As you seek the Lord and repent of any wrongdoing, the Lord will forgive you (1 John 1:9). The Lord will enable you to move forward; He will heal your heart of regret (Ps. 34), and His mercies (Lam. 3:20–23) will sustain and strengthen you in your journey

Weeping endures for a night, but joy comes in the morning (Ps. 30:5). Rejoice! God is a mender of wounded hearts. Remember, God greatly loves you, and you are never alone in your journey (Heb. 13:5b). He will never let His children journey alone.

> *Dear Lord,*
> *Thank You for the freedom and healing that I have in You and You alone, for You are my shelter and rescuer in the pain of my regret. Thank You, Lord, for being my strength, comforter, and for rescuing me in the midst of my wounded emotions. Father, thank You for Your endless love and hope, for in You I find peace.*

Chapter 15

DEPRESSION

Lord, Be My Song in the Night

...weeping may endure for a night, but joy cometh in the morning.
—Psalm 30:5b

Many have asked if I suffered with depression when my son passed. By God's wonderful grace, I did not suffer with depression. As I respond to their questions, I remember the Lord's strong presence as He held me very closely; He carried me until the storm passed over.

On the fateful day of Victor's journey home, the Lord carried me. I can only describe this like the security a child feels who sits in her father's lap as he holds and carries her. His sweet and peaceful presence was my shelter and sustaining hope. Yet, there were days when the longing for my precious son was great. At times, the grief was as piercing as it had been on the day of his passing. God my sustainer enabled me to process this pain with His hope and strength and move on. One day at a time...

Though weakened by the reality of the passing of my gentle giant, the Lord sustained me with the strength of His presence. The Lord's presence continues to be my sustainer and my healer; He continually reminds me of His great love for me, never once leaving or forsaking me (Heb. 13:5b). And as the days and months and years pass, my Heavenly Father continues to be my peace of mind, my strength, my stronghold; and my very present comfort.

Today, because of God's great love, I am lovingly held in the presence of His peace; I am never alone for my Heavenly Father carries me in His great and mighty love.

> Dear Lord,
> Though my heart and emotions are clouded by the pain of sorrow, Father, I trust You, for You are my anchor of hope. You will continuously be my loving grace, turning my night of weeping into a joyous morning. I love You, Lord, for You are my everlasting hope (Ps. 30:5b).

Yet, many through their journey of grief have suffered or are suffering with depression. Often, these emotions are like a revolving door of an array of emotions. Yet with many as they exit through the various stages of emotional healing, the impact of these emotions lessens. There would be weeks of great longing for my gentle giant, and God Almighty would lift the sorrow of grief from me with the sweet assurance that I will see my son again. But God! He is the healer of wounded emotions; He heals our broken heart and binds up our wounds (Ps. 147:3).

God see our tears, heals our wounded heart; and gives us great joy (Ps. 30:5). The Bible says that God gives us strength in our weakness (2 Cor. 12:9) and gives us peace (John 14:27). We each journey differently in our grief, and for some, depression has been a part of that journey.

God met Elijah in his fear and depression at a time when he felt alone. God is faithful, and His children never journey alone. Although Elijah did not suffer the loss of a loved one, he suffered a loss of faith during a time of tremendous trial. During Elijah's turbulent emotional struggle, he, like many, became overwhelmed with sorrow and fear and became hopeless and depressed! In sorrow, one may feel, at times, hopeless, alone, or afraid. Some may isolate themselves, feeling that no one cares and struggling to believe that God cares, just as Elijah struggled.

But God is faithful in our journey of life when it seems hopeless, when we are alone, or in a time of depression. As we see in life of Elijah, God never leaves His children.

As we read about Elijah, we will see that he became greatly discouraged in his journey of life. But we will also see how God encouraged and strengthened him, giving him hope in the journey. God reminded him that he was not alone.

Please read First Kings 19:

> And Ahab told Jezebel all that Elijah had done, and withal how he had slain all the prophets with the sword.
>
> Then Jezebel sent a messenger unto Elijah, saying, So let the gods do to me, and more also, if I make not thy life as the life of one of them by tomorrow about this time.
>
> And when he saw that, he arose, and went for his life, and came to Beersheba, which belongeth to Judah, and left his servant there.
>
> But he himself went a day's journey into the wilderness, and came and sat down under a juniper tree: and he requested for himself that he might die; and said, It is enough; now, O Lord, take away my life; for I am not better than my fathers.
>
> —1 Kings 19:1–4

After Jezebel heard that Elijah had killed all the prophets of Baal with the sword, she proclaimed her revenge against Elijah. Elijah became afraid and ran for his life. After fleeing, he left his servant in Beersheba, went a day's journey into the wilderness, and sat under a juniper tree. In his hopelessness and fear, he prayed to die.

Again, the emotion of depression affects individuals differently. Depression is often characterized by a deep sense of hopelessness and despair. Some may describe depression like living in a dark place of loneliness and defeating emotions. When sudden, tragic circumstances enter our lives, we may begin to lose hope. Like Elijah, hopelessness or depression can lead to despair.

QUESTIONS

► Are you struggling with emotions that cause you to despair of life? If so, please describe:

_____

_____

_____

► Do you feel forsaken and alone? If so, please describe:

_____

_____

_____

► Are you struggling with hopelessness or depression? If so, please describe:

_____

_____

_____

► If so, do you feel that your depression will overwhelm you? Please describe:

_____

_____

_____

▶ Do you feel that your emotion of depression is greater than the help and intervention of God's strength and power? (Isa. 41:10) If so, please describe why:

_____

_____

_____

> And as he lay and slept under a juniper tree, behold, then an angel touched him, and said unto him, Arise and eat.
> And he looked, and, behold, there was a cake baken on the coals, and a cruse of water at his head. And he did eat and drink, and laid him down again.
> And the angel of the LORD came again the second time, and touched him, and said, Arise and eat; because the journey is too great for thee.
> And he arose, and did eat and drink, and went in the strength of that meat forty days and forty nights unto Horeb the mount of God.
> —1 KINGS 19:5–8

God met Elijah at the very point of his fear, depression, and hopelessness. The Lord sent an angel to provide him with food. The angel encouraged Elijah to eat in preparation for a forty-day's journey.

Many struggle, seeking relief and hope from the crushing weight of depression. But God met Elijah when his discouragement had deepened into despair, and He met him at the point of his essential needs. He gently provided Elijah with both food and rest.

Rest is very important in the journey of grief. A lack of ample rest may hinder your emotional healing. Also, the lack of rest may increase your depression and / or anxiety. Let God minister to you in this area as He did for Elijah.

> I will both lay me down in peace, and sleep: for thou, Lord, only makest me dwell in safety.
> —PSALM 4:8

QUESTIONS

▶ Did God meet Elijah at his point of need? If so, how?

_____

_____

_____

▶ Did God meet Elijah in his time of depression and despair? If so, how?

_____

_____

_____

▶ Did the Lord comfort Elijah? If so, how?

_____

_____

_____

▶ Did the Lord provide rest for Elijah? If so, how?

_____

_____

_____

▶ Did the Lord provide strength for Elijah? If so, how?

_____

_____

_____

Often when we are weary from the battles of life (sorrow, depression, fear, discouragement, pain), we struggle to see God's provision. We may struggle to believe that the Lord will give us victory (John 16:33). The battle is amplified by our fears, insecurities, and doubts. But God is greater than our fears and insecurities, for He is God Almighty, and there is surely nothing impossible with God (Luke 1:37).

Though our emotions scream run, flee, or hide when hard battles and trials come, we must remember that our Lord, who deeply loves us, will find us in our place of hopelessness. God is faithful, and He is able! God rescues and heals His wounded children!

> And he came thither unto a cave, and lodged there; and, behold, the word of the Lord came to him, and he said unto him, What doest thou here, Elijah?
>
> And he said, I have been very jealous for the Lord God of hosts: for the children of Israel have forsaken thy covenant, thrown down thine altars, and slain thy prophets with the sword; and I, even I only, am left; and they seek my life, to take it away.
>
> —1 Kings 19:9–10

In the midst of Elijah's struggle, God met him. He had fears and questions, as we do, and God met him there—as He meets us. God cares about the struggles, fears, and heartaches of His children (Ps. 34). We can trust the Lord with our wounded emotions and sorrow (Ps. 37:3–5).

After Elijah arrived at Horeb, he came to a cave and he lodged there. Sometimes, one's struggling emotions can represent a cave of loneliness and the darkness of depression and wounded emotions.

Questions

► Have you felt as though you were living in a cave with a prolonged, painful emotion of depression? Please explain:

_____

_____

_____

► Has your depression become your constant companion? Please explain:

_____

_____

_____

- ▶ Did Elijah make his concern known to the Lord? How?

- ▶ When your heart is troubled, do you make your concerns known to the Lord? If yes, please explain:

- ▶ Does God hear our prayers? If yes, please explain:

- ▶ Please share a time that the Lord answered a great prayer request for you.

- ▶ Do you seek the Lord with your concerns, fears, heartache, and sorrow?

  Yes

  No

▶ If so, do you find comfort in the Lord as you seek Him?

_____

_____

_____

> And he said, Go forth, and stand upon the mount before the Lord. And, behold, the Lord passed by, and a great and strong wind rent the mountains, and brake in pieces the rocks before the Lord; but the Lord was not in the wind: and after the wind an earthquake; but the Lord was not in the earthquake:
>
> And after the earthquake a fire; but the Lord was not in the fire: and after the fire a still small voice.
>
> And it was so, when Elijah heard it, that he wrapped his face in his mantle, and went out, and stood in the entering in of the cave. And, behold, there came a voice unto him, and said, What doest thou here, Elijah?
>
> And he said, I have been very jealous for the Lord God of hosts: because the children of Israel have forsaken thy covenant, thrown down thine altars, and slain thy prophets with the sword; and I, even I only, am left; and they seek my life, to take it away.
>
> —1 Kings 19:11–14

What an awesome and loving God! As Elijah, a troubled man, stood on the mountain, the strong winds tore into the mountains and broke the rocks. But God was not in the wind! There was an earthquake and a fire—and still God was not there. But then there was a still small voice, and Elijah knew it was the Lord. God asked Elijah, "What are you doing here, Elijah?" In great fear and discouragement, Elijah brought his concern before the Lord.

QUESTIONS

▶ How has the Lord met you at your point of brokenness and depression?

_____

_____

_____

> Have you struggled in your emotional pain, believing that God has forsaken you? If yes, please explain:

_____

_____

_____

Have you brought your innermost struggles before the Lord, yet wondered if He would answer and truly cared? God cares for and loves you. God cares about every tear that falls from your eyes; you are not alone, dear one (Zeph. 3:17).

> In your struggle to believe that God would intervene in your depression have you given up hope?

Yes

_____

No

_____

(Remember, depression is often characterized by overwhelming emotions of despair, hopelessness, and defeat. Also, with continuous, despairing emotions of depression, one may have thoughts of suicide. At times, there are those in this journey who may need the intervention of counseling from a professional, biblically-based counselor.)

> And the LORD said unto him, Go, return on thy way to the wilderness of Damascus: and when thou comest, anoint Hazael to be king over Syria: and Jehu the son of Nimshi shalt thou anoint to be king over Israel: and Elisha the son of Shaphat of Abelmeholah shalt thou anoint to be prophet in thy room. And it shall come to pass, that him that escapeth the sword of Hazael shall Jehu slay: and him that escapeth from the sword of Jehu shall Elisha slay. Yet I have left me seven thousand in Israel, all the knees which have not bowed unto Baal, and every mouth which hath not kissed him.
> —1 KINGS 19:15–18

After Elijah brought his complaint before the Lord; the Lord answered him. The Lord instructed Him to return to the wilderness of Damascus, and a new journey began in his life. To Elijah's great amazement, the Lord informed him that He had reserved seven thousand in Israel who had not bowed their knees and worshipped Baal. He was not alone, after all.

What blessed and joyous news to hear that seven thousand had not bowed to the gods of Baal! When Elijah felt forsaken and alone, God ministered to his essential needs and then to the heart of His servant. The Lord never left Elijah alone because the Lord never leaves His children alone in their journey of life.

The Lord truly heals depression and our broken hearts. He will restore joy to the heart of the one who grieves. God is faithful! Great is God's love for you! Those who truly have the blessed hope of salvation have the blessed joy of reaching a hurting, lost, and dying world with the blessed hope of eternal life.

Suddenly God answered Elijah and revealed His plans and purpose for Elijah's life (Jer. 29:11–13). What an amazing God we serve! He knows the heartache, depression, and the deepest concerns of our heart. He understands, better than anyone, the sorrows of our heart. What an awesome God we serve!

God never leaves His children in a state of hopelessness and despair; He will meet us in our pain of grief. Remember, God heals the grieving heart. He *never* leaves His children to journey alone.

▶ How has the Lord ministered to you in your emotional pain of depression?

_____

_____

_____

▶ Has the Lord answered you suddenly in your journey of grief? If yes, please explain:

_____

_____

_____

> Blessed be God, even the Father of our Lord Jesus Christ, the Father of mercies, and the God of all comfort; who comforteth us in all our tribulation, that we may be able to comfort them which are in any trouble, by the comfort wherewith we ourselves are comforted of God.
>
> —2 Corinthians 1:3–4

Depression

God is faithful and will use every part of your journey of grief for His glory as you journey with Him. God can also use us to minister to others!

▶ Has the Lord used you to minister to another individual in their journey of grief? If so how?

_____

_____

_____

▶ How has God's faithfulness in your life strengthened you?

_____

_____

_____

▶ Have you used God's faithfulness and strength in your life to strengthen others in their journey of grief through His Word? If yes, please explain:

_____

_____

_____

▶ Has God's faithfulness encouraged you to encourage others? If yes, please explain:

_____

_____

_____

▶ Has God's faithfulness and strength given you hope and enabled you shared this hope with others? If yes, please explain:

_____

_____

- Has the Lord used your journey to draw you into a deeper relationship with Him? If yes, please explain:

_____

_____

_____

- Has embracing God's faithfulness and strength enabled you to "press on" (2 Cor. 12:9)? If yes, please explain:

_____

_____

_____

- Have you embraced, or are you learning to embrace God's love and His Word that you are never alone (Heb. 13:5)? If yes, please explain:

_____

_____

_____

Dear one, God greatly loves you. I know that at times you may struggle to believe that He does because of the trauma of the passing of your loved one. God is greater, however, than the sorrow and lack of faith you may be struggling with. He greatly loves you. The pain that you are experiencing is not greater than the Lord's love and care for you. Depression for many a grieving heart is like a heavy clothing of despair, hopelessness, and darkness. But God! He never, no never, leaves His children to journey alone. The Lord loves you with an everlasting love (Jer. 31:3), and He will strengthen you and give you hope.

You are precious to the Lord, and your heart will not forever be troubled and broken. Our Heavenly Father is surely a mender of broken hearts. The depression that you may encounter will surely one day cease, and there will again be a song on your lips as the Lord sings over you with songs of rejoicing (Zeph. 3:17; Ps. 42:8).

You will again have hope. Take one day at a time as our Heavenly Father holds you close. One day this life will pass, and we will forever be in the glorious presence of our Heavenly Father, embracing those who are His and have passed from this life to eternity. Rejoice! Dear one, the "best is yet to come" (1 Cor. 2:9).

Father,

I rejoice that You are my hope. Thank You, Lord, that You go before me, and I need not be afraid or dismayed. You, Lord, are my hiding place; Your peace, hope, and strength carry your children to safety, through the storm to the other side (Deut. 31:8).

Chapter 16

PERSEVERANCE

Lord, Be My Strength as I Seek to Move Forward

But verily God hath heard me; he hath attended to the voice of my prayer.
—Psalm 66:19

Prior to Victor's home-going, I was scheduled to go to a particular country, and I prayerfully waited for that day. Unbeknownst to me, God had an appointed time for my precious son's home-going (Heb. 9:27). One-and-a-half months after Victor's death, I woke with my hands lifted, crying out to the Lord, "Lord, I miss Victor." The Lord spoke to my heart, "Rita, do you want to be with Victor or complete the journey?" I then said to the Lord, "I want to complete the journey."

Because the Lord sent me to that particular country, an extension of Hope Unlimited Ministry began there. Hope Unlimited Ministry is a ministry for single-parent families and others in need, providing a host of Christ-centered services here in the United States. The ministry is also located in various countries internationally. During those days, the Lord held me very close to His heart, just as He does now. I felt in the first days after Victor's home-going that the Lord had placed me in a room where only He and I dwelled; there He held me, gently wiping every tear from my eyes. He comforted me with His love, His Word, and the overwhelming presence of His peace.

The Lord ministered to the very core of my longing and grieving emotions. The Lord met these needs as no one else could. It was Jesus Christ and He alone who ministered healing in my life beyond what anyone else could imagine. Praise the Lord! I purposed by His grace that until my last breath I would serve Him, reaching a hurting, lost, and dying world with the good news of salvation—God's redeeming power through His Son Jesus Christ.

Many struggle with the emotions of despair and want to give up in the midst of their pain. The Lord desires to reach us where we are—in the deepest core of our emotions—and bring healing and hope.

Dear Lord,

My life and hope is in You. Thank You, Lord, for Your strength, mercy, and love that has enabled me to persevere and press on. Thank You, Lord, that I never journey alone, for You never leave us. You enable us to move forward in the plans and purposes that You have for our lives.

In order to experience full healing, we must be willing to surrender, trusting the Lord and totally allowing Him to have control of our lives. Perhaps we have struggled with pain, depression, anger, and hopelessness for years; nevertheless, God is able to heal us and set us free from the bondage of our wounded emotions.

You may ask, "How do I release my grief and heartache to the Lord?"

1. Please pray and seek the Lord.
2. Go honestly before the Lord and tell Him your struggles.
3. Become transparent before the Lord and tell Him of any anger, bitterness, or emotional pain.
4. Become transparent before the Lord and tell Him of the anger you have over your loved one's passing.
5. Become transparent before the Lord and tell Him of your fears and insecurities due to your loved one's passing.
6. Cry out to the Lord and ask for strength.
7. Please seek the support and prayers of others.

God sees and knows all things concerning you (Ps. 139:1–18), and He will heal you in your journey of grief. God is faithful! Though it seems that the loneliness, tears, and sorrow will never cease, God cares for you. Weeping endures for a night; your joy will come again (Ps. 30:5).

TRUST GOD

You can rejoice, for your sorrow will one day pass and your joy will come again. In your sorrow and weakness, trust the Lord! Life will have new meaning, for God will give you hope and joy as He travels with you in the journey of life. Remember, weeping endures for a night, but joy comes in the morning.

▶ Are you struggling to move on? Please describe your struggle:

Does it become a greater struggle each day to summon the strength to move on? Please explain:

(Excerpt: *My Journey Home: Jesus Christ the Rescuer of Wounded Emotions*)

Do you feel like giving up? Your journey of depression may be a season of churning emotions. But God is able and will deliver you. He will heal the pain that you may be struggling with and will restore your joy. Please know that you are greatly loved and that God is your healer and strength (Ps. 61:2; 17–19). He will never leave or forsake you. Though your journey may be one of weariness and depression, know that God is faithful and the weeping you may be experiencing will pass. Your joy will come. (Ps. 30:5)

> Hear my cry, O God; attend to my prayer. From the end of the earth I will cry to You, when my heart is overwhelmed; lead me to the rock that is higher than I.
> —Psalm 61:1–2, NKJV

▸ Does God hear your cry?

Yes

No

Please explain:

Yes, God does hear your cry, for He hears the cries of the faint-hearted. God loves you and does answer prayer! You are not alone; the Lord will enable you to heal in your grief and persevere in the journey of healing (Ps. 61:1–2).

- Do you believe that the Lord hears your prayers and will help you in your sorrow?

If yes, please explain:

If no, please explain:

God greatly loves you and will forever love you (John 3:16). God cares about the tears that you cry (Ps. 30:5); you are not alone (Heb. 13:5).

From the end of the earth I will cry to You…
—Psalm 61:2, nkjv

- Have you cried out to the Lord in your sorrow? Please explain:

- Have you felt like giving up? Please explain:

...for he hath said, I will never leave thee, nor forsake thee.
—Hebrews 13:5

- Does the Lord provide hope and strength for His children when they feel despairing and emotionally wounded? Please explain:

- Do you personally believe that the Lord will forever love His children? ("Jesus Christ will forever love you"; John 3:16)

    Yes

    No

    Please explain:

- Is God a merciful and loving God?

    Yes

    No

If no, please explain:

> ...lead me to the rock [Jesus Christ] that is higher than I.
> —Psalm 61:2, NKJV

- Who is the Rock?

- Why should we be led to the Rock, Jesus Christ, in our sorrow?

- Is the Rock your strength, sustainer, and hope? Please explain:

- Will Jesus Christ; the Rock, enable us to persevere in our journey of grief? Please explain:

God greatly loves you; He is the Rock that we come to in our journey of grief. God is a mender of wounded hearts and our sustainer of our peace. God does not leave us to journey alone. God cares about every tear that falls from your eyes. God sees and knows, and He will be your anchor in the storms of life. You are wonderfully made, and God has a plan for your life (Ps. 139:1–18). You are greatly loved!

Many have asked me, "But Rita, how did you move forward?" My reply was, "Day by day, and step by step with the Lord and His tremendous grace, love, mercy, and strength." There were mornings when I awoke knowing that I was unable to move forth in His will for my life unless He moved mightily on my behalf. In the early journey of Victor's home-going, at times the reality of His passing was like a tidal wave at high seas crashing to shore.

But God was my stay, holding and strengthening me in the storm and enabling me to press on. The Lord continues to sustain me with a beautiful strength as He lovingly and faithfully journeys with me. You may ask, "How can I possibly move forward after the passing of my loved one?" God will meet you in the very depths of your fears, pain, and hopelessness. He will bring *hope*.

God will comfort you and help you process your pain, grief, and despair through His love and His Word. As I sought the Lord in prayer, He truly comforted me. I sought His Word for hope to move forward, and I was surely sustained and strengthened. The Lord's love in the hearts of His children embraced me with compassion and many prayers. Yes! There are times even today as I write that I miss my handsome son and his smiling face. Yet I rejoice that our separation is not final; I will surely see Victor, my gentle giant, again never to depart (2 Cor. 5:8).

God who is faithful beyond measure rescues His children in their grief as they struggle to press on (Phil. 3:13–15). And in the midst of the emotions of grief, God prevails and strengthens us (Phil. 4:13). He never leaves His children alone (Heb. 13:5)!

> *Dear Lord,*
>
> *Truly, You are an awesome God! Today I sing Your praises with songs of rejoicing and hope. Thank You, Lord; by Your wonderful grace and matchless power, I journey with You as You hold me closely in Your love, mercy, and grace. Lord, truly You are an awesome God. You enable me to persevere by Your loving grace!*

Chapter 17

PURPOSE

Does My Life Have Purpose?
The Void and Emptiness of the Passing of a Loved One

"For I know the plans I have for you," declares the LORD, "plans to prosper you and not to harm you, plans to give you hope and a future."
—Jeremiah 29:11, NIV

After the home-going of my son, my gentle giant, I wondered if my life ever be the same. I wondered if my laughter would be as joyous, my smile as wide, my giggle as gleeful. I would often detour around our favorite restaurants and the places that he and I used to visit. The void of his presence I experienced would bring tears as I traveled to the places that once were our places of laughter. But God! He began to lovingly heal those places of grief. Victor and I had often enjoyed one restaurant that served a variety of delicious foods; we spent many occasions there, laughing and enjoying our fellowship. Months after Victor's home-going, I visited our special restaurant, and as I ate my salad, I wept. But as the months passed, the tears lessened as God continuously began to fill the great void in my heart with His comfort. He assured me that He would never leave me alone, and He tenderly ministered to my grieving heart.

God has been my hope and redeemer, always reminding me in a loving, quiet voice that He was with me—as the days turned into weeks, and the weeks into months, and the months into years.

> *Dear Lord,*
> *Thank You, Lord, for Your faithfulness and love as You lovingly journey with Your children. Thank You, Lord; You have purpose (Jer.29:11–14) in my sorrow. Though my heart yearns for the embrace of my precious loved one, You, Lord, will fill my void with Your love. Thank You, Lord, for holding me until the storms of sorrow passes over.*

QUESTIONS

- Are you struggling in your grief and the void of your loved one's passing? If yes, please explain:

_____

_____

_____

- Are you seeking the Lord to heal and fill the emotional void of your loved one's passing? Please explain:

_____

_____

_____

- Have you determined that your life's journey will be one of a life of hopelessness? Please explain:

_____

_____

_____

Please read Jeremiah 29:11–13:

> For I know the thoughts that I think toward you, saith the Lord, thoughts of peace, and not of evil, to give you an expected end. Then shall ye call upon me, and ye shall go and pray unto me, and I will hearken unto you. And ye shall seek me, and find me, when ye shall search for me with all your heart.

Now let's look at those verses individually:

> For I know the thoughts that I think toward you, saith the Lord, thoughts of peace, and not of evil, to give you an expected end.
>
> —Jeremiah 29:11

▶ What are the thoughts that God thinks about you? Please explain:

_____

_____

_____

▶ What kind of future does God desire for you? Please explain:

_____

_____

_____

> Then shall ye call upon me, and ye shall go and pray unto me, and I will hearken unto you.
> —Jeremiah 29:12

▶ Have you called upon the name of the Lord for help and hope in your pain and sorrow? Please explain:

_____

_____

_____

▶ Have you prayed to God who is mighty to deliver those who call upon His holy and mighty name? Please explain:

_____

_____

_____

▶ Are you struggling in despair in a disarray of emotions of hopelessness? Please explain:

_____

_____

_____

▶ As a Christian, are you struggling in a whirlwind of emotions, seeking to fill the void in your heart with other things outside of Jesus Christ? Please explain:

_____

_____

_____

Only God can reach the core of our emotional wounds and give us hope. God will heal those emotions, fill the void in our heart, and strengthen us in our despair and brokenness. God will surely turn our weeping into *joy* beyond measure (Ps. 30:5b). Yes! God will be our constant companion in our pain (Ps.40:2).

You are not alone! The pain of emotions that you may be feeling will not destroy or defeat you. God who is mighty to deliver will deliver you. You are not hopeless, for the "God of hope" loves you, sees your pain, and will set you free from the turbulence of emotions. Trust God; He is faithful and able to give you hope.

> Then shall ye call upon me, and ye shall go and pray unto me, and I will hearken unto you.
> —Jeremiah 29:12

▶ What does the Word say that the Lord will do when we call upon His name and pray?

_____

_____

_____

▶ Please write *five* examples of God answering the prayers of His children in the Bible.

1. Scripture:

_____

Answered prayer:

___

2. Scripture:

Answered prayer:

___

3. Scripture:

Answered prayer:

___

4. Scripture:

Answered prayer:

5. Scripture:

Answered prayer:

And ye shall seek me, and find me, when ye shall search for me with all your heart.
—Jeremiah 29:13

▶ Please explain what God meant when He said, "You will find Me when you search for Me with all your heart."

▶ Should God's children search for Him with all their heart? Why?

▶ Are you seeking the Lord with all your heart? Please explain:

The Lord hath appeared of old unto me, saying, Yea, I have loved thee with an everlasting love: therefore with lovingkindness have I drawn thee.
—Jeremiah 31:3

Do you believe that God greatly loves you with an everlasting love? Yes! He loves you deeply, and you are never alone. You are so loved by our Heavenly Father! In the journey of grief, with a painful heart of emptiness, you may cry out, "Does my life have purpose?" Your life does have great purpose, and God knows the pain and the emptiness that may arise in your heart.

The Lord has not left you alone; it is He who will surely heal the grief in your heart. God sees every tear that falls from your eyes and every longing of your heart (Isa. 41:10). God sees you, and you are never alone (Heb. 13:5). He is a Rock for His children (Ps. 61:1–2). Dear one, as your journey of healing continues with the Lord, you will be strengthened by His grace, and your hope will be restored.

God's mercy is new every morning, and His faithfulness is great (Lam. 3:20–23). God's faithfulness and mercy will sustain you in the deepest struggle of your grief, and His grace will carry you moment by moment, day by day. *Your weeping may endure for a night; but your joy will come in the morning!*

Dear Lord,

Though I cannot see beyond my today, my hope and purpose are in You. Thank You, Lord—You alone fulfill our deepest longing and pain with Your great love, understanding, and healing. Thank You, Lord, for never letting Your children journey alone.

Lord, I trust and love You (Prov. 3:5).

Chapter 18

PEACE

Lord, You Are My Peace

Peace I leave with you, my peace I give unto you: not as the world giveth, give I unto you. Let not your heart be troubled, neither let it be afraid.
—John 14:27

God is truly faithful, and He does care. The day of Victor's home-going was a day of great unexpectedness and disbelief. I could not believe that just a short time earlier I had embraced my son and prayed with him. But God comforted me with the great power of His presence and His Holy Word. During the first two days after Victor's home-going, the Lord gave me three scriptures:

> We are confident, I say, and willing rather to be absent from the body, and to be present with the Lord.
> —2 Corinthians 5:8

> And as it is appointed unto men once to die, but after this the judgment…
> —Hebrews 9:27

> But I would not have you to be ignorant, brethren, concerning them which are asleep, that ye sorrow not, even as others which have no hope.
> —1 Thessalonians 4:13

You are not alone. God's peace will sustain you through the storms of life and enable you to press on in the darkest nights. The Lord will help you to emerge from the storms of life without feeling abandoned and shipwrecked. God will safely bring you through to the other side of healing. *Praise the Lord!*

YET…

In my sorrow, God surrounded me with His steadfast love and peace that surpasses all understanding. I felt like I was in a room surrounded by His great love, grace, and strength. This peace dwells in my heart today when the yearning for my son or the battles and trials of life are before me. God's love, peace, and strength have journeyed with me steadfastly and faithfully as He often carries me in the journey of life. Oh! How my heart greatly praises my great God! What an awesome God we serve!

Thank You, Lord, for embracing us with your peace as the storm of grief passes over. Thank You, Lord, that Your peace is greater than the storms of life as Your peace calms my heart and mind and gives me great hope. Lord, Your peace gives me courage to trust You as You enable me to press on to the other side of my healing…

QUESTIONS

▶ Do you struggle you to find peace with the passing of your loved one? Please explain:

_____

_____

_____

Peace I leave with you, my peace I give unto you: not as the world giveth, give I unto you. Let not your heart be troubled, neither let it be afraid.
—John 14:27

Peace I leave with you, my peace I give unto you…

▶ Who gives us peace? Please explain:

_____

_____

_____

▶ What does this peace mean to you? Please explain:

_____

_____

_____

- ▶ Have you personally experienced this peace that God gives during your journey of life and in this season of grief? Please explain:

___

- ▶ Please describe this fellowship of peace with the Lord. If you have not experienced this peace, are there any hindrances to experiencing this peace? If so, what are the hindrances and struggles?

___

Not as the world gives, give I unto you…

- ▶ What temporary peace does the world give? Please explain:

___

- ▶ Does the temporary peace of this world give sustaining peace and hope? Please explain:

___

Let not your heart be troubled…

- ▶ What does the Lord mean when He says, "Let not your heart be troubled"? Please explain:

___

- Is your heart troubled? If yes, please explain:

- Does the Lord care about your troubled and broken heart? Please explain:

- Does the Lord desire to rescue and heal you and others in their troubled emotions? Please explain:

...neither let [your heart] be afraid.
—John 14:27

- What freedom does a person feel when he or she is no longer fearful or troubled by the despair of grief? Please explain:

PEACE: FEAR AND ANXIETY

▶ Are you walking in God's peace, or are you struggling with fear and anxiety? Please explain:

_____

_____

_____

▶ Does the pain of grief overwhelm you? If yes, please describe:

_____

_____

_____

▶ Are you struggling to have peace? If yes, please explain:

_____

_____

_____

▶ Does your life seem to be in a dark tunnel of despair? If yes, please explain:

_____

_____

_____

In the darkest of nights, God is greater. God is light in the midst of the darkest night. He is our hope though it may seem that sorrow will prevail. Do not fear; our God always prevails and brings victory to His children.

▶ Please write five scriptures that relate to God's promises of peace:

_____

_____

Using the five scriptures that you chose, please write how these scriptures relate to God's promises of peace.

- ▶ God's promise: Scripture 1:

- ▶ God's promise: Scripture 2:

- ▶ God's promise: Scripture 3:

- ▶ God's promise: Scripture 4:

- ▶ God's promise: Scripture 5:

Often when one is overwhelmed by grief (Ps. 61:2), life may seem to be like living under a dark cloud or in a dark tunnel. God truly is your answer for the pain, depression, loneliness, and despair that you may be living in. He will hold you close and heal the grief that you may be encountering.

The Lord will journey with you step by step; He will help you to process your grief. As you allow the Lord to heal you, His grace and strength will enable you to move forward. How, you may ask? God will carry us through to the finish! God is faithful and will heal your grieving heart and restore your peace within.

God's peace surpasses the peace that the world gives (John 14:27); His peace will sustain you through your journey of grief. He will heal every emotional pain that you may be enduring. God is faithful beyond measure! He will give your life purpose! You may struggle now with wondering if your life has purpose. With a resounding *yes,* I can tell you: God has purpose for your life; He has a wonderful plan for your life! (Jer. 29:11–13)

As we cry out before the Lord, giving Him our pain, anguish, fears, and deepest longings (Heb. 4:16), He will hear our cries (Ps. 30:5b) and surely heal our wounded emotions. There are no quick fixes in the journey of grief; however, God's sustaining power can carry you through one day at a time. Yes, one day at a time.

He will bring you through your journey into a deeper and more intimate relationship with Him. Though there may be seasons of longing to see and embrace your loved one once again; remember, He will carry you through until you reach the other side of your journey of healing. Yet, until this time, seek the Lord with all your heart and draw deeply into the comfort, healing, love, and peace of our Heavenly Father. You are not forsaken or abandoned as one without hope or peace. Remember, God never leaves His children alone.

> Now may the God of hope fill you with all joy and peace in believing, that you may abound in hope by the power of the Holy Spirit.
> —ROMANS 15:13, NKJV

Dear Heavenly Father,
How great You are, Almighty God, who reigns mightily in the sorrows and heartache of Your children. Thank You, Lord, for You are our Abba Father, our peace and sustainer in our journey of life. Thank You, Father, for the sweetness of Your love as You journey with us from this life to life eternal.

Chapter 19

REFUGE AND COMFORT

Lord, You Are My Refuge and Comfort

From the ends of the earth I call to you, I call as my heart grows faint; lead me to the rock that is higher than I.

—Psalm 61:2, NIV

My Heavenly Father is my great refuge, my place of comfort and hope. In Him alone, I found my greatest strength when my precious gentle giant passed from this life to life eternal. Others told me that I was in shock, but my Heavenly Father gave me a promise that I would not grieve without hope, nor would I grieve long in my journey of healing (1 Thess. 4:13).

God carried me as I grieved as one journeying from grief to hope. With God as my refuge, each day was a day of strength; the Lord held me closely, and my days of grieving were embraced with peace and calmness. Though I grieved, God's refuge was my sustainer and peace, and God's strength greatly prevailed in the midst of my journey of grief. In my journey of grief, I would feel an overwhelming sense of loss and longing for my son's presence. Yet, God lovingly provided me with strength greater than my own and would clothe me with immeasurable peace and comfort.

God has continued to strengthen me as He alone enables me to continue reaching a hurting, lost, and dying world with the priceless gift of salvation which is only found in Jesus Christ the Messiah. Yet, the Lord who is my refuge and my rest continues to "stir in my heart" the cry of the perishing who are lost without the gift of eternal life, seeking hope in a perishing world. I am thankful and rejoicing as I rest in the refuge of peace and strength that God Almighty gives me.

YET...

As the Lord becomes our refuge, a place of comfort in our grief, we can rest in Him. His faithfulness and strength enable us to journey forward in life. Also, we can trust God's Word because God's promises are faithful, and in His promises, we will surely find comfort and a wonderful refuge of hope. As we trust in the Lord, we will find He is truly our sustaining peace (John 14:27) that perseveres and is unchanging in the trials, battles, or heartaches of life.

God gives our lives purpose (Jer. 29:11), and His grace and strength enable us to fulfill His divine will for our lives.

> Dear Lord,
> Thank You for being a refuge and comfort in the life of Your children. Your love Lord shelters me in the comfort of Your presence (Ps. 107:29). Your Word strengthens me with mercy and grace as You are my refuge and comfort (Lam. 3:21–23).

As I continue in life's journey, God's hope, love, peace, and strength continue to encourage me with the precious hope that I will see Victor again. God's awesome love greatly comforts me with the promises of His Word.

God Is Our Hope

- Do not be afraid (Isa. 41:10).
- May the Lord sing over you with songs of rejoicing (Zeph. 3:17).
- God is your peace (John 14:27).
- God's mercy will sustain you every morning (Lam. 3:21–24).
- God will "never leave or forsake you" (Heb. 13:5).
- God is your strength in fear (Isa. 41:10).
- God is your provider: Jehovah Jireh (Phil. 4:9).
- He is the God of impossibilities (Jer. 32:27).
- God has a plan for your life (Jer. 29:11–13).

The Lord desires to be our comfort in our sorrow and grief. He desires to be our refuge—a place of shelter and a place of peace. He can and will be our refuge as we trust and rest in Him, knowing that He is faithful and will never leave or forsake us.

> For in the day of trouble he will keep me safe in his dwelling; he will hide me in the shelter of his sacred tent and set me high upon a rock.
>
> —Psalm 27:5, niv

QUESTIONS

- Do you have a place of refuge and comfort with the Father? If so, describe your place of comfort with Him.

- If you do not have a place of comfort with the Heavenly Father, are you struggling with hopelessness? Please explain:

- If you do not have a place of comfort with the Heavenly Father, are you struggling with unrest? Please explain:

- If you do not have a place of comfort with the Heavenly Father, are you struggling with despair? Please explain:

- What is your greatest struggle in finding comfort and rest with the Heavenly Father? Please explain:

God knows and sees the pain of your struggle; please know that you are not alone. The Lord will embrace us where we are even in the greatest struggles of our lives as we trust Him. You may say, "My faith is weak"; God will not forsake you, but will meet you in your weakness. Run to the Lord though your heart may be struggling with emotions that you cannot define. God knows, and He deeply loves you, dear one. Because of God's great love and care we can fully rest in Him. Remember, God desires to journey with you and comfort you in your grief.

- Please describe what "resting in God" means to you.

_____

_____

_____

- What scripture relates to resting in God?

  Scripture:

_____

- What is your greatest struggle or fear in resting in Jesus Christ and the comfort He desires to give you? Please describe:

_____

_____

_____

The greatest strength and comfort that a Christian can embrace is trusting Jesus Christ in the trials and battles of life. The Lord will be your constant companion and strength in your journey; you are not forsaken or abandoned.

- Please describe God's *comfort*:

_____

_____

_____

Refuge and Comfort

▶ What scriptures relate to God's comfort?

Scripture:

_____

Scripture:

_____

God is faithful! He will give you peace and comfort, for His mercies are new every morning, and His compassions fail not!

▶ Please describe *peace*:

_____

_____

_____

▶ What scriptures relate to God's peace?

Scripture:

_____

Scripture:

_____

God provides hope to those who feel hopeless and afraid. Please allow God Almighty to be your hope and strength through your journey of grief and healing.

▶ Please describe *hope*:

_____

_____

_____

▶ What scriptures relate to God's hope?

Scripture:

_____

Scripture:

_____

God greatly loves you! His love will strengthen you and heal the areas of your heart that may be wounded.

▶ Please describe *strength*:

_____

_____

_____

▶ What scriptures relate to God's strength?

Scripture:

_____

Scripture:

_____

God's love will persist in the darkest storms of your life. You are not alone, and the Lord will surely enable you to persevere by His love and strength.

▶ Please describe *perseverance:*

_____

_____

_____

▶ What scriptures relate to God's perseverance?

Scripture:

_____

Scripture:

_____

Trust God who is faithful beyond measure. God will not fail or forsake you! God is faithful to His promises and will journey with you in the storms of life.

▶ Please describe what it means to trust God:

_____

_____

_____

▶ What scriptures relate to trusting God?

Scripture:

_____

Scripture:

_____

God is your refuge and shelter in the time of need. Are you trusting Him to shelter you in the storms of grief? Please trust God, dear one.

▶ What scriptures relate to God being a refuge—a place of shelter from the trials, pain, and sorrows of life?

Scripture:

_____

Scripture:

_____

▶ Please describe God being our refuge:

_____
_____
_____

God hears the prayers of His children and is merciful to those who do not know Him as Lord and Savior. Trust God in faith, believing that He knows your needs and will provide for you.

▶ Please describe *faith*:

_____
_____
_____

▶ What scriptures relates to God's faithfulness?

Scripture:

_____

Scripture:

_____

God loves you and has a plan and purpose for your life. Please trust Him; our Heavenly Father loves you greatly, and His ways are perfect.

▶ Please describe what "God has divine purpose for His children's lives" means to you:

_____
_____
_____

▶ What scriptures relates to God's purpose in your life?

Scripture:

___

Scripture:

___

Remember, God greatly loves you. He will forever journey with you, giving you hope, mercy, and strength along the way.

▶ Please describe what this promise, "the Lord will never leave or forsake us," means to you:

___

___

▶ What scriptures relates to this promise?

Scripture:

___

Scripture:

___

Allow the Lord to heal you in the midst of the turbulent emotions you may be pondering in your heart. The greatest strength and comfort that Christians can obtain is by trusting Jesus Christ in their fears, trials, battles, and the journey of grief. While the journey may be different for each individual, no one can succeed without Jesus Christ journeying with them in their grief. He is truly the healer of wounded emotions.

Many struggle to believe that God is able to help them move on with their lives after the passing of a loved one. They struggle in their grief and wounded emotions. Often, sadly, throughout their lifetime, they are burdened and broken with questions and a heart of bitterness, despair, depression, anger, and loneliness.

God is faithful, and His love and healing is deeper than the deepest sorrow.

God can reach us in the pain of our sorrow. Please let Jesus Christ be your refuge and hope today. God will *not* fail you in your journey of healing as you trust Him. The Lord will lovingly be your faithful and dearest companion. He will strengthen you in the journey, giving you hope, peace, and healing. You will again smile, and the laughter in time will come. Remember, God still has purpose for your life, and He will complete the work that He has started (Phil. 1:6). God will not fail you, dear one.

Dear Lord,

Thank You, Lord. You are my hiding place, a refuge in the journey of grief. Lord, thank You for being my song in the night (Ps. 42:8) and comforting me in my sorrow. Thank You, Lord, for being my beautiful refuge of comfort, love, and strength, journeying with me as You heal my broken heart.

Chapter 20

JOY BEYOND MEASURE

Lord, You Are My Joy

Weeping may endure for a night, but joy comes in the morning.
—Psalm 30:5b, nkjv

How can I express the joy that God has given me in the midst of what many would call the greatest trial of my life? The Lord has provided joy immeasurable, peace beyond measure, and strength that I am unable to define. Oh, what joy surrounds my heart like a medley of music resounding in the depths of my heart! Oh, with what joy and strength my Heavenly Father has sustained my life and my total being as I continue life's journey in God's awesome and loving faithfulness. As I breathe and live, the Lord continuously holds me and surrounds me with whispers, "Daughter, I am here," affirming that I am never alone. Oh! Words cannot express our Heavenly Father's love and His awesome faithfulness, yet I live and embrace His marvelous grace.

> *I praise You, my Heavenly Father, for You have never left me alone in the journey of my healing, in the journey of my grief. For You, Lord God, embrace and hold me close, and I am never alone. Father, thank You that Your children are never alone. Your promises are true that You, Lord God Almighty, will never leave us alone. Oh Father, my mouth sings Your majestic praises. What an awesome and faithful God You are, my Heavenly Father, Daddy. And one day I will see You face to face…face to face.*

Please look up these scriptures regarding our joy:

1. Psalm 63:4–8
2. Psalm 81:1
3. Psalm 42:1–4
4. Psalm 66:1–2
5. Psalm 98

6. Psalm 105:1–5
7. Psalm 16:11
8. Psalm 35:27
9. Psalm 43:4

After the passing of a loved one, many people have asked if joy will ever return again. The answer is "yes," as we trust the Lord. God's faithfulness restores our hope and joy. God is faithful even when we are faithless (2 Thes. 2:13). Furthermore, we need never walk alone on this journey of healing—no matter what stage of grief we are in, no matter how vibrant or faded our hope. The Lord will never leave or forsake us (Heb. 13:5). For some, the process of healing may consist of breakthroughs in healing as well as setbacks of loneliness and sadness. But be of great joy, the Lord God is your overcomer, and He will strengthen you in the journey of your healing. *As we journey in our healing, Abba Father encourages us in the midst of our grief. Be encouraged!*

Please look up these words of encouragement from the Lord:

1. Isaiah 61:3
2. Lamentations 3:20–23
3. John 14:27
4. Isaiah 51:11
5. Zephaniah 3:17
6. Luke 1:37
7. Isaiah 41:10
8. Psalm 30:5b
9. Jeremiah 32:27
10. Psalm 42:8
11. Nehemiah 8:10
12. Isaiah 43:1–2

▶ What do these scriptures mean to you? Please explain:

_____

_____

_____

_____

_____

- ▶ Do you believe that God is able to do what He has promised in these scriptures?

    Yes
    _____

    No
    _____

As the Lord journeys with us in our grief, there are times when we may struggle with sadness instead of joy. But, with each valley of sadness, the joy will come again (Ps. 30:5b).

- ▶ Do you struggle at times with having joy and believing that these scriptures are true for your life? If so, why?

    _____

    _____

Often in the journey of grief, emotions may seem like a revolving door. But God is a healer and greater than these emotions.

> Ye are of God, little children, and have overcome them: because greater is he that is in you, than he that is in the world.
> —1 John 4:4

- ▶ Does the emotion of hope in your life seem like a revolving door? If so, please explain:

    _____

▶ Does it feel at times that all hope is lost without your loved one? Please explain:

Moving forward is not easy; it is not without tears or loneliness—yet God's joy remains in the midst of our tears. During the process of grief, our emotions may change from day to day, but God's grace will enable us to become stronger in the journey. God will surely carry us safely to the other side of healing.

Often when a loved one passes, the loss of their presence and love is grievous. Some angrily blame God for their loved one's passing. Yet the Lord can and will sustain His children and show mercy to their grieving hearts. God's love, grace, and strength will enable you to press on and have hope in your season of grief. The truth is we live in a fallen world, and every individual is born as a sinner. But Jesus Christ came so that a hurting, lost, and dying world might have eternal life with Him if they choose to receive His free gift of salvation.

But, there is a great hope for those that remain. Moreover, those who truly have the blessed hope of salvation now have the blessed joy of reaching a hurting, lost, and dying world. As we seek to reach the world with this blessed hope, they too can have eternal life.

Oh Lord, I rejoice in Your presence as Your love embraces me. You are my song in the night (Ps. 42:8).

JOY BEYOND MEASURE

In the journey of grief, my greatest joy is knowing that my son knows Jesus Christ as His Lord and Savior and I will surely see Him again (John 3:16).

A couple days after my gentle giant's home-going I drove down the street where the horrendous accident happened. As I drove, sadness filled my heart. Suddenly, the Lord told me to praise Him. I began to praise God that Victor was saved and had eternal life with Him. I then began to praise the Lord that He had saved *me*.

As his mother, I was able to instruct him as the Holy Spirit had instructed me; He gave me great wisdom to pass on to him and my other children.

I praise the Lord that Victor loved Him and lived for Him. I rejoice that Jesus Christ is his Savior and that he rejoices and lives with Jesus Christ today.

Oh Lord!

Thank You for being my joy in the midst of my sorrow. Even in the moments when I long for my precious son, Your presence surrounds me with peace and joy. Even in my tears I have hope. Thank You, Lord.

Chapter 21

OUR GOD REIGNS!

For if we believe that Jesus died and rose again, even so them also which sleep in Jesus will God bring with him. For this we say unto you by the word of the Lord, that we which are alive and remain unto the coming of the Lord shall not prevent them which are asleep. For the Lord himself shall descend from heaven with a shout, with the voice of the archangel, and with the trump of God: and the dead in Christ shall rise first: Then we which are alive and remain shall be caught up together with them in the clouds, to meet the Lord in the air: and so shall we ever be with the Lord. Wherefore comfort one another with these words.

—1 Thessalonians 4:14–18

Rejoice, oh you saints! Our Redeemer lives, and we too will one day reign with Him for eternity never to depart. We will reign with Him in the wonderful presence of His peace and grace. Surely, there will be no more tears or sorrow; there will forever be peace and joy, and we will reign with our Heavenly Father forever more! Rejoice, oh you saints, for our Redeemer lives!

Dear Lord,
Thank You, for You have been my joy in sorrow and my mighty anchor of hope. Lord, I praise and thank You, for You are a mighty, awesome, and faithful Messiah!

God's Faithfulness as My Journey Continues

It seems like yesterday that my precious son and I were sitting at the kitchen table laughing about the day's events. It all seems like yesterday. But there is coming a day when I will feel Victor's loving embrace once again. Until that time, by God's grace, I press on to serve my Heavenly Father with all my heart, strength, and breath. Yet, Jesus Christ, my faithful companion, forever journeys with me.

God alone has healed my grieving heart. He has taken the pain of grief and truly given me hope. Though there are moments of yearning for my son and for the sight of my Savior's face, I am comforted and restored in His presence.

By God's awesome grace, as a servant in ministry, I continue to travel within the US and overseas. God reminds me that there is a hurting, lost, and dying world perishing without the hope of Jesus Christ. So until I breathe my last breath I will, by the grace of God, continue to reach the world so they will have the hope of eternal life through Jesus Christ.

One day I will surely inhale for the very last time, and I will see my gentle giant Victor for all eternity, never to depart. I will see my Savior face to face in the presence of His glory. What a day of rejoicing that will be! Until eternity, Lord, may I be found faithfully serving and reaching a lost, hurting, and dying world (Matt. 28:1–20).

> *Daddy, thank You for Your faithfulness and saving my son Victor. Thank You that You are his Messiah and he lives with You today. Thank You that this life will pass, and I will see my gentle giant again for all eternity. Lord, I will see your face, and I pray that I will hear you say, "Well done, My good and faithful servant." I love you, Victor. I love You, Daddy: Thank You for saving Victor and giving him eternal life! (John 3:16)*
>
> *Lord, until that time, I pray that You enable us to finish the race with excellence. Help us to reach a hurting, lost, and dying world with the glorious gift of salvation.*

For God so loved the world, that he gave his only begotten Son, that whosoever believeth in him should not perish, but have everlasting life.

—JOHN 3:16

The Lord will forever love and journey with you. Jesus Christ greatly loves you and desires that you spend eternity with Him forever. What a blessed gift of salvation God has given those who receive His Son as their Lord and Savior. What joy to know that as you pass from this life your life will be caught up eternally with God Almighty.

If you do not know Jesus Christ as your Lord and Savior, please receive Him today. I have again enclosed the beautiful plan of salvation that you may truly know Him as Lord and Savior.

(Excerpt: My Journey Home: Jesus Christ the Rescuer of Wounded Emotions)

- First: God loves you (Rom. 5:8–9).
- Second: All have sinned (Rom. 3:10–12, 23).
- Third: Sin separates us from God (Rom. 6:23).
- Fourth: God desires to be your Heavenly Father and spend eternity with you (Rev. 3:20; John 1:12; 3:16).

You may ask how you can have this relationship with God through Jesus Christ our Lord:

1. Repent of your sin (Acts 3:19).
2. Believe that Jesus Christ died and rose again that you can have eternal life (John 3:16; 15:13).
3. Repent and receive Jesus Christ as your Lord and Savior. Ask Him to come into your heart as Savior (John 1:12; Rom. 3:20).
4. Allow Jesus Christ to rule over your life (Gal. 2:20); He will do amazing things in your life.

Lord Jesus Christ, please forgive me of my sins, save my soul, and give me eternal life. I believe that You died on the cross for my sins and were resurrected again that I may have eternal life. I repent of all my sins. Please, Lord Jesus Christ, come into my heart and become Lord of my life. Take total control of my life; I surrender (Gal. 2:20) my life to You. Thank You, Lord Jesus Christ, for Your love in receiving my prayer and saving my soul. In Jesus' name, I pray. Amen.

ABOUT THE AUTHOR

God's love and faithfulness endures forever...

Many years ago, the Lord began to prepare me for ministry, as He had gently affirmed in my heart that one day I would be in ministry. Prior to the calling of ministry, I worked as a Tennessee coordinator for Families in Action, which is located in Jackson, Tennessee. I was also a director for a state-funded program as the Director of Primary Prevention, a prevention / intervention program for youth. While employed in this position, I worked as a consultant for juvenile court. Later, I was employed at Fortwood Mental Health Center, where I worked as a counselor. I continued to work for this agency until the Lord opened the door for me to work in full-time ministry.

I have served on various committees such as a state steering committee for intervention and prevention, a volunteer board committee for the Department of Corrections, Chattanooga area task forces, Scenic City Women's Network, Race Reconciliation Committee (seeking to encourage Christians to minister to others outside of their cultural boundaries), and various other committees. Also, I developed the Inmate Speaker's Bureau program through the Department of Correction and the Early Elementary Intervention Program.

I have a bachelor's degree in organizational behavior, a master's degree in education, and a doctorate degree in Christian counseling. I am a licensed counselor through the Tennessee Board of Mental Health and Mental Retardation and a board-certified professional counselor through the American Psychotherapy Association. Also, I am clinically certified through the College of Forensic Counselors as a cognitive behavioral therapist and a domestic violence counselor. I am also nationally certified as an alcohol and drug counselor (NAADAC).

In 1997, the Lord birthed Hope Unlimited Ministry through my life and called me into full-time ministry. Praise the Lord, Hope Unlimited Ministry, as an international ministry, is located in various other countries. Also, Hope Unlimited Ministry, as a ministry for single mothers and children, offers many services to single-parent families, ministries, and agencies. Hope Unlimited Ministry provides various ministry services such as Christ-centered life skills and other Christ-centered ministry services. These services are provided at no cost.

As a servant of Jesus Christ, I lovingly, through Him as His vessel, seek to be the hands and feet of Jesus Christ. The heart of the vision for Hope Unlimited Ministry is to reach these families and a hurting, lost, and dying world for Jesus Christ that they may be saved.

CONTACT THE AUTHOR

Please visit the author at:

Website:
http://www.hopeunlimitedministries.org

Email:
myjourneyhome@epbfi.com